"Dean Register personifies the m a dynamic communicator of b leaders who know him, Dean who maintains a high standard of excellence in leadership creativity.

Dr. Reggie Ogea
Director, Jim Henry Leadership Institute
Professor, Leadership & Pastoral Ministry
New Orleans Baptist Theological Seminary
New Orleans, LA

"If you want to read a book on how you can honor God with day-to-day, grind-it-out faith-filled Christian living, then <u>Holy Grit</u> by my friend Dean Register is absolutely the message for you."

Tim Wildmon, President
American Family Association &
American Family Radio

"I absolutely love how M. Dean Register, my pastor, and spiritual father for over 35 years, can take deep, Biblical truths and teach them in a way that all of us can understand and apply to our lives. I hope and pray that <u>Holy Grit</u> inspires you, as it did me, to draw closer to Jesus and to keep fighting the good fight of faith."

Jonathan Howes
Lead Pastor of Graystone
church and Co-Host of
Family Goals Podcast with
David Pollack and
Pastor J

"The drumbeat of a pastor's heart reverberates through the pages of <u>Holy Grit</u>. This is a much-needed message of hope distilled through the lives of Bible heroes. It's the best I've read on the necessity of perseverance."

Jim Henry, Past President, of Southern
Baptist Convention, Pastor Emeritus of First
Baptist Church, Orlando, FL, Contributing
Editor of <u>Preaching Magazine,</u> and author
of numerous books including <u>The Two
Shall Become One</u>, <u>The Pastor's Wedding
Manual,</u> and <u>Keeping Life in Perspective</u>

HOLY GRIT

THE WILL TO PERSEVERE

M. DEAN REGISTER

WESTBOW
PRESS®
A DIVISION OF THOMAS NELSON
& ZONDERVAN

WestBow Press books may be ordered through booksellers or by contacting:

WestBow Press
A Division of Thomas Nelson & Zondervan
1663 Liberty Drive
Bloomington, IN 47403
www.westbowpress.com
844-714-3454

ISBN: 978-1-6642-9935-1 (sc)
ISBN: 978-1-6642-9936-8 (hc)
ISBN: 978-1-6642-9934-4 (e)

Library of Congress Control Number: 2023908360

Print information available on the last page.

WestBow Press rev. date: 06/01/2023

CONTENTS

DEDICATION

To Sharon:

My wife, the love of my life since we were kids in school. Your name should be on the cover of this book for many reasons. Mainly because you personify loving Jesus with holy grit better than anyone I know! Forever and a day!

To Heather:

My beloved daughter. Wife to Cord and an amazing mother to six. You are pure sunshine. You make life overflow with joy and compassion and a sprinkle of mischief. Your perseverance always inspires me!

To Wes:

My treasured son. Husband to Nicole and a wise daddy to Walker. Serving and leading Crosspoint with you has been the delight of my ministry. Your fire for Jesus invites others to abandon the cold and discover His warm embrace.

To my Grandchildren:

Jeremiah, Ellie, Saddler, Judson, Josiah, Walker, and Gideon. Your Papa adores you! May you follow Jesus with holy grit forever. Gaudium de veritate!

ACKNOWLEDGMENTS

First and foremost, I owe a gigantic debt of gratitude to my executive ministry assistant, Robyn Smith. She has typed everything I have published for the past twenty-seven years. She radiates grace and faith. I wish every pastor in America had an assistant with a heart like hers. She and her husband, Terry, are a magnetic couple who never fail to encourage believers.

I am deeply thankful to the churches in Brunswick, GA; Enon, LA; Franklin, NC; Gulfport, MS; and Hattiesburg, MS, who gave me the honor to be their pastor.

Furthermore, to Westbow Publishing, a division of Thomas Nelson/Zondervan, you have made the process rewarding with your expertise and guidance.

INTRODUCTION

Quitting is trendy today. On the backside of the Covid pandemic, millions of people quit a career, quit school, quit marriage, quit church, quit the ministry, or quit a job. Anthony Klotz, a professor of Management at Texas A&M University coined the phrase "The Great Resignation" to emphasize the magnitude of the worldwide movement. Obviously, many factors contribute to quitting. Some are legitimate and necessary. Some are sad and bad. But, what if instead of quitting for the wrong reasons, we began a perseverance movement for the right reasons? What if we decided to live with holy grit? What if we discovered life lessons from prominent leaders in the Bible who overcame long days of adversity, exhaustion, exasperation, and discouragement?

A. W. Tozer counseled that "the only book that should ever be written is one that flows from the heart, forced out by the inward pressure."[1] This book didn't have to be published. It did have to be written. In many ways, it is my story of struggling, often failing, but striving to face adversity with godly audacity. This is not a book for chest beaters who boastfully scale spiritual mountains. It is not a quick read for impulsive achievers eager for an adrenalin fix. Instead, I have written for ordinary plodders who wrestle with God's will. For mere Christ-followers who endure meltdowns, battle misery, and experience messiness. For backroom believers who dare to beg God for holy perseverance when their flesh pants for sinful appeasement.

I am neither an expert in the art of overcoming nor am I exempt from the trauma of being overwhelmed. I am familiar with both. I come to you timidly but with decades of experience drenched in two four-letter words considered obscure by some and obsolete by others. The two words are "holy grit." I have often asked the question, "What is my duty, my obligation to Christ?" I am so indebted to His grace and forgiveness that I am determined to persevere for His glory. Allow me to clarify what I mean by "holy grit."

Angela Duckworth explained in her masterful book, *Grit: The Power of Passion and Perseverance*, that success in the field of education, sports, military training, or business is driven by a unique combination of passion and perseverance, more than talent and IQ.[2] A peer review meta-analysis of 127 studies and two field studies affirmed Duckworth's data and concluded that "perseverance without passion isn't grit, but merely a grind."[3] She stated, "To be gritty is to invest day after week after year in challenging practice. To be gritty is to fall down seven times and rise eight."[4]

Holy grit is the process of working out the salvation that God worked in us. Some seasons of life feel more like a persevering grind than a passionate glide, but I'm not referring to human effort to earn salvation. I'm not advocating any kind of meritorious action to win God's favor. I am pleading for followers of Christ to persevere passionately because He is worthy. I agree with Jerry Bridges that "God has made it possible to walk in holiness. But He has given us the responsibility of doing the walking."[5] The gift of grace does not nullify the importance of effort and obedience. It enables and sustains grit.[6] Jesus invites us into a life of holy grit and makes it clear that we will face tribulation. He also offers us outrageous joy because He overcame sin and death. His overcoming makes it possible for us to be overcomers.

When my son played Little League baseball, I coached his 12 yr. old team. We had a scrappy group of players with lots of talent, except for one kid. I'll just call him William. At 5'10" and 185 lbs, he was easily the biggest guy on our team. He was also the least coordinated and the most awkward. On the first day of practice, I quickly realized that William lacked basic dexterity. I instructed the boys to select a partner and warm up their arms by tossing a baseball back and forth. In the meantime, I emptied the bats and helmets from a duffel bag. Within five minutes I heard a muffled cry coming from William, and I asked him what was wrong. "Well coach, I was holding my glove out by my side, and my partner didn't throw it into my glove. He hit me in the chest." A teammate nearby burst out laughing. At that moment, I knew that coaching William would require a unique blend of instruction and motivation. I said, "William, I want to teach you how to move your glove to catch the ball so you won't get hurt." "Okay, thanks coach," he whimpered.

Soon, however, everyone on our team made a concerted effort to help William. They loved his positive attitude, even if he couldn't catch a grounder or hit a pitch. When the opening game of the season approached, I was concerned that William's skill was so deficient that he might get injured. I talked to his parents, and they shared the same concern. His mom informed me that he had never played baseball, but he merely wanted to be part of a team. William personified sportsmanship. He served as our cheerleader from the bench during every game. He never missed a game, but he never wanted to bat in a game. William struggled with a phobia. During practice, I tried everything I knew to keep him from bailing out of the batter's box. I sought advice from other coaches. Nothing worked. I threw unlimited pitches and promised him endless milkshakes and hamburgers if he would stay in the batter's box and swing his bat. Nevertheless, William always bailed out before the pitch arrived.

Our last game of the season found us facing the number-one team in the league. They boasted a strong pitcher who fired 70 mph fastballs and used a nasty sidearm pitch that fooled good hitters. A baseball traveling 70 mph at a Little League distance from the pitcher's mound to home plate is equivalent to a pitch speed of 93 mph at a Major League distance. I knew we would need to play our best game to beat them. We patched together a couple of runs due to the other team's errors, and the score was tied as we came to bat in the bottom of the last inning. Our first batter walked. The next batter hit an infield dribbler and raced to first base beating the throw. Our third and fourth batters struck out. Our best player kept the rally alive, hitting a sharp line drive that bounced off the glove of their shortstop, advancing the runners. So now the bases were loaded, but we had two outs. William stood in the dugout, yelling encouragement. I stood in the coach's box near third base. We desperately needed a hit.

It was the last game, and William had never batted. I weighed the risk and called for William to grab a helmet and find a bat. With a bewildered frown across his face, he asked, "You mean me, coach?" William shuffled toward the batter's box with his head down. The pitcher smirked as William fretfully stepped to the plate. In a blink, the pitcher went into his windup and released a fastball. Before it arrived, however, William bailed out of the batter's box. "Strike one," the umpire bellowed. I clapped my hands and shouted, "Swing the bat, buddy. Don't bail out on me." The pitcher glanced at his coach and fired another fastball. Once again, William bailed out as "strike two" sounded. I called time out and walked toward him. I knew he was feeling overwhelmed. "You can do this, William," I emphasized. "There's no shame if you swing and strike out. The honor lies in your grit to stay in the batter's box whatever the outcome. So don't bail out." I wish I could adequately describe the metamorphosis that began. William nodded at me confidently and then stepped back into the batter's box. He kicked the dirt, digging a secure place for his feet. That was something I had never seen him do. He shifted his weight toward his back leg. He waggled his bat as if to say, "Come on. Throw your best stuff!" I was stunned to watch the transformation. I studied the pitcher as he gripped the ball. When he began his windup, I noticed his pitching hand drop low near his hip to sidearm the throw. My anxiety heightened.

William could get hurt! In seemingly slow motion, I shouted, "Look out, William! Duck!" as the ball sailed toward his head. My exhortation and the ball arrived at the same second. William didn't budge as the ball slammed into his shoulder. The umpire thundered, "Take your base!" William trotted to first base rubbing his shoulder as the winning run crossed home plate. Our players instantly mobbed an elated William. It was an unforgettable moment as the sun settled beneath the amber and pink clouds of a summer evening. I gathered our equipment and walked toward an exit gate.

Holy grit is a devout passion to live out the abundant life that Jesus worked in us without giving up.

William was walking with his parents a few paces ahead. He stopped, turned around, and said, "Coach, I didn't bail out on you. I showed some grit, didn't I?" I put my arm around him and labored to hide the tears.

In a peculiar way, I identified with William. I saw myself in his struggle. I wondered how often I had bailed out on Jesus. I thought about all the times I wanted to honor the Lord but chose to stay in the dugout and watch the action from a safe distance. I felt convicted. It was a holy awakening. I sensed the Lord saying, "Don't bail out on me, Dean. Regardless of how hard Satan fires misery and mayhem, don't bail out! No matter how anxious you are about the high and tight pitches of failure and fear, show holy grit. Persevere and be an overcomer."

The memory from that event years ago remains adhesive. Sometimes on quiet evenings when I'm alone with the Lord, I am reminded to practice holy grit and persevere through trials. Holy grit is a righteous resolve. It is a devout passion to live out the abundant life that Jesus worked in us without giving up. The value of holy grit rests with our tenacity to trust the Lord to accomplish His purpose in all the tangled complications of life.

A few years before C. S. Lewis became a follower of Christ, a colleague invited him to attend an academic fellowship organized by J. R. R. Tolkien. It was called the "Kolbitors." Lewis's attention was riveted by the name of the fellowship, and he remarked that it sounded Norse. The colleague replied, "It's Icelandic for 'coal-biters'. It means those who sit so close to the fire they can almost bite the coals."[7]

So, I invite you to join me as we draw close to the fire of God's truth. Let's fan the flame together. If we prefer not to bite the coals, we can still experience the heat of a burning passion to persevere with holy grit.

CHAPTER 1

Teach us, O Lord, the discipline of patience,
for to wait is often harder than to work.

Peter Marshall

Those who wait on the Lord shall
renew their strength...

Isaiah 40:31 (NKJV)

Mold me and make me Lord, after thy
Will while I am waiting yielded and still.

Adelaide A. Pollard

Abraham: Enduring a Severe Wait

Waiting doesn't come naturally for me. I fidget. I drum my fingers. I bounce my leg when confined to a chair. I pace and take deep breaths. I live in the house of ASAP. I'm not sure the waiting gene ever developed in the double helix of my DNA. If waiting is a virtue, then I confess that I am often bad. I like quick fixes. I prefer immediate solutions to complicated problems and especially desire instant answers from God.

I'm embarrassed to admit that I growl at my computer when it's slow. I'm not alone in confessing my impatience. Researchers examined the viewing habits of over six million internet users and found that people can't wait more than a few seconds for a video to load. After five seconds, the abandonment rate is twenty-five percent. After ten seconds, half the viewers have left the site.[1] The negative side of technology compels us to seek instant gratification and neglect appropriate patience. So, I wonder, "How did Abraham embrace such a severe wait? How did an ancient nomad living in a culture of idolatry endure the slow torturous passage of time with relentless faith in God's promise?"

First Steps of Obedience

Abraham was seventy-five years old when he received God's call. He seemed more like a retiree than a potential pioneer for building a nation. He lacked the qualifications of a founding father. He didn't look like a heroic patriarch.

Future historians may refer to him as "the father of the faithful." They may extol his gritty obedience. They may laud him as a holy risk-taker. But when Abraham emerges on the pages of Scripture, he is nothing like that. He was comfortably nestled in Haran. As far as we know, he was not looking for God. God, however, looked for and found Abraham, and everything about his life changed from that moment forward.

Isn't it intriguing that God calls the unqualified in order to qualify them? Isn't it startling that God graces the undeserving so that they might bless others? Isn't it significant that the first steps of faith can become a tipping point of impact on future generations?

If Abraham wanted to go with God, he couldn't remain where he was. A break from his comfortable and familiar surroundings required a breakthrough of trust in God. The city of Haran, like the city of Ur, abounded with cultic rituals. Both places were prominent centers of moon worship where fertility gods took priority to satisfy devotees.

God's first words to Abraham necessitated a change so that he could enjoy the promised blessing. God said, "get out," and Abraham "went out." Abraham's response revealed a raw faith evidenced by bold obedience. The faith-extolling chapter eleven in the Book of Hebrews states that he "went out not knowing where he was going."[2] Would it have been rude for Abraham to ask God to be more specific? Put yourself in Abraham's sandals. How eager would you have been to inform your family and friends that you were going with God somewhere to an uncertain place merely because God said you should?

Mission assignments and great exploits of faith today require detailed planning, keen analysis, and accurate GPS calculations regarding the topography of an area. Would we censure Abraham if he had paused to request more clarity from God? Hear me out. I'm not suggesting that careful planning and visionary strategy are insignificant. Organization and implementation are vital to intentional effectiveness. I'm just trying to wrap my mind around what kind of faith drives a person to believe in God with total abandon.

That's one reason I hold such a deep admiration for Abraham. It's also the reason why I feel rebuked by his simple steps of faith. Abraham dared to believe God. He believed God was sufficient for whatever happened to him. Abraham trusted an unknown future to God. No reluctance. He believed God would fulfill His promise. Pure surrender. God was sufficient! I find his obedience refreshingly uncorrupted. Can you relate to such sincere devotion? Can you remember a time when you stepped beyond predictability and threw yourself into God? Do you recall trusting God more than you worried about your circumstances? When was the last time your faith was ten times as big as your fear?

As I leaf through the pages of my life, I wish they revealed a splendid chart of faith that rises higher and higher. Instead, I see a graph of several ups and many downs, zigzagging across the years. I have often craved a robust faith. The kind that flexes muscles to stop bullets of doubt. The kind that hurdles obstacles of discouragement and despair. I long for a sturdy faith that refuses to yield to temptation, one that perseveres no matter how grueling the battle.

Nevertheless, when I analyze Abraham, the trailblazer and champion of faith, I discover a different dimension. I notice that between his initial steps of faith and the final confirmation of his faith, he embraces a severe wait. Abraham's faith does not portray a blustering bravado.

Biblical faith is never a tidy leap from one spiritual peak to another. It is more like a marathon through a perilous valley of bedlam peppered with messy delays and long intervals of wait training.

He never struts with a smug holiness. On the other hand, he gives no hint of faultless and easy devotion. Biblical faith is never a tidy leap from one spiritual peak to another. It is more like a marathon through a perilous valley of bedlam peppered with messy delays and long intervals of wait training.

Worship While You Wait

Abraham's first activity upon entering Canaan was to build an altar for worship. An altar represented his desire to consecrate himself to God. It served as both a memorial to mark a profound encounter with the Lord as well as a sacrificial surrender. Initially at Shechem and later at an undisclosed location between Bethel and Ai, Abraham engaged in worship by calling upon God. The Hebrew word for Bethel means "house of God," and the Hebrew word for Ai means "place of ruin."

Waiting can make us feel like we are caught somewhere between ruin and godliness. Like we are stuck in uncertain territory flanked by hallowed ground on one side and desolate wasteland on the other side. Time grinds to a halt when we are forced to wait. A tug of war erupts. We experience the protracted pain of a present delay pulling against the ecstasy of future hope.

Waiting gnaws at our faith and feeds upon our patience. But if we are wise, we will listen for the whisper of God as He bids us to be still while He moves. Waiting is more than what God does "to us." It is what God does "in us." God is working in our waiting ever how displaced and overwhelmed we are.

Waiting is our opportunity to seek Him in spirit and truth. God invades our waiting when we surrender to Him in worship. There is no doubt that Abraham handled a heavy work schedule. He had tents to erect, water to secure, and livestock to feed and protect. He had tools to sharpen and repair, wood to gather, fires to tend, and food

Desperation can be a catalyst for holy grit and intimate worship.

to cook. Through it all, Abraham made worship a priority. He was busy, but he didn't allow his work to replace his worship.

I think Abraham worshiped while he waited for a couple of reasons. First, he longed for intimacy with God. He needed to hear God's counsel in order to fortify his faith. He passionately desired close communion. Desperation can be a catalyst for holy grit and intimate worship. According to Scripture, spiritual intimacy is not a cryptic art shrouded in mysterious rituals. All true intimacy is cemented in a faith relationship. God takes pleasure in our faith, and without faith, we can neither be close to Him nor can we ever please Him. Ironically, intimacy grows best in times and places that force us to cling to God. Abraham found himself in a strange land, facing fresh challenges and coping with new fears. Consequently, drawing close to God in worship was non-negotiable. It was crucial to Abraham's survival.

Second, Abraham pursued God's guidance through prayer. He called upon the name of the Lord. Prayer involves a shameless appeal to God! When our hearts cry out for God's instruction, we realize that waiting can be a fruitful season. My flesh might resist asking directions from God. But when I worship Him through the discipline of prayer, He plans my steps and my stops.

I wrote a devotional on the subject of prayer for an evangelical news journal some years ago. Several months later, a church member informed me that I was quoted in a *Reader's Digest's* section, "Points to Ponder," regarding my statement on prayer. Sure enough, sandwiched near Martin Luther King Jr. and Robert Penn Warren was this conviction I hold about prayer:

"Essentially, prayer is based on a relationship. We don't converse freely with someone

Waiting gnaws at our faith and feeds upon our patience.

we don't know. We bare our souls and disclose our hidden secrets only to someone we trust."[3]

I still contend that prayer is not a technique we perform. It's a relationship we treasure. The deeper our love relationship with Christ, the more dynamic our prayer life becomes. Corporations pay huge sums of money for consulting. According to comprehensive industry research, US companies spent nearly $330 billion on consulting in 2022.[4] Numbers of that magnitude are staggering, but they represent the priority companies place upon acquiring the best guidance and direction. Prayer is a type of consultation. It is offered to us by the infallible God of the universe, and it is free. Through prayer, we can receive His perfect management of our lives. We can trust Him through grueling snail-paced days and dark desolate nights of waiting. His Word is sure and unfailing when we call upon Him.

So as you wait, don't hesitate to go to God "asking." He will answer you. Don't neglect to go to Him "seeking." He will find you. Never forget to go to God "knocking." He will gracefully open a door for you.

Beware of Snares

Enduring a severe wait is peppered with peril. Subtle snares are hard to detect and harder to discern. Hidden in the shadow of our waiting lies a trap of self-sufficiency. I grew up in a culture of emotional

Enduring a severe wait is peppered with peril. Subtle snares are hard to detect and harder to discern.

and spiritual autonomy. I learned to champion independence to my own detriment, and I incurred the painful consequenc~~ of my decisions. Thankfully, God disciplined me to real~

holy grit and self-sufficiency are not compatible. They are fierce rivals competing for our allegiance as we wait. Self-sufficiency tempts us to reach for easy solutions and take detours contrary to God's will. The siblings of self-sufficiency are impatience and impulsivity. They clamor for our attention today much like they did for Abraham when he faced three unexpected crises of faith.

His first crisis involved the lure of a comfortable environment. Who can hurl a stone of criticism at Abraham for wanting better circumstances when a famine settled upon Canaan?

We are not being honest with ourselves if we casually assume we would have managed the crisis better than he did. Perhaps some individuals could give themselves a passing grade for surviving a famine, but I'm sure I would have flunked in that environment. Who, with a measure of sanity, enjoys the prospect of starvation? There is nothing wrong with preferring the tranquility of plenty rather than the tyranny of hunger. The ever-present lure of temptation, however, beguiles us to crave comfort at the expense of godliness. It coaxes us to leverage our preferences above God's pleasure.

During my adolescent years, I relished hearing missionaries speak in our church. I soaked up their stories about faith, hope, and love. My idealism was shattered, however, by an emphatic reply given by one missionary to the benign question, "Do you enjoy your work?" He stared at the floor, collecting his thoughts in awkward silence. The congregation waited for his answer. Firmly but tenderly, he replied, "No, I don't enjoy being separated from my family and familiar surroundings. I don't like the loneliness. I disdain ⌐ ⌐rivation. I hate the threats from antagonists. But if I ⌐esus what I feel like doing, then my comfort will ⌐mission." Ouch. I wasn't expecting the gentle ⌐ a grand slam. His truth scored big. I sat in my ⌐is reply and evaluating how my preference for ⌐ my faith.

When Canaan began to resemble a famished land, Abraham "went down" to Egypt. Those two words indicate more than a geographical direction. They reveal a spiritual descent. Abraham swallowed the lure of a comfortable environment. He chose not to wait upon God. There is no evidence that he consulted with God to receive the "go" signal. By leaving the place God had assigned, he unwittingly imperiled his faith and jeopardized his wife.

Did he interpret the parched ground as a sign that God was unable to sustain him? Did he travel to Egypt because he questioned God's goodness? Perhaps he jumped to the false conclusion we often embrace when our waiting mingles with adversity. We wrongly assume that God's purpose should not test the status of our trust. We conclude that waiting for His timing is too arduous. Consequently, we look for the places that are least discomforting and most appealing.

Fear often breathes so close to faith that it infects belief with doubt.

A second crisis soon confronted Abraham. As he approached Egypt, his anxiety peaked. He faced the temptation of a panic-driven escape. Fear often breathes so close to faith that it infects belief with doubt. Abraham worried about the Egyptians. He feared they might kill him to abduct his wife. He quickly contrived a plan. He persuaded Sarah to tell the Egyptians that she was his sister instead of his wife. It was a clever half-truth because Sarah was the daughter of Abraham's father through another woman. The ploy succeeded much better than Abraham imagined. Little did he realize that Pharaoh's officials might invite her to share the Egyptian ruler's bedroom. Pharaoh gave Abraham camels, oxen, and sheep. He also gave him a team of servants in exchange for Sarah. Abraham's scheme backfired. It was a recipe with all the ingredients for a catastrophe. The entire redemptive covenant teetered on the slippery slope of disaster. Who can speculate the dreadful outcome if Pharaoh had impregnated Sarah?

Of course, we have the advantage of looking back at the biblical record and knowing how it all turned out. But neither Abraham nor Sarah had that benefit. They were the flesh and blood participants in a real-life dilemma.

We often exploit our advantage by looking at biblical characters from a convenient distance. We feel at ease analyzing and criticizing their decisions. We become armchair evaluators reclining with an arrogant detachment of chronological superiority. It's like viewing the D-Day invasion of Normandy in a relaxing movie theatre. We watch the soldiers hit the beaches and scale the fortified cliffs while we hold a soft drink in one hand and popcorn in the other. However, for the soldiers who were there, who saw the sand turn red with blood, who experienced the thunderous explosions and the withering barrage of gunfire, it was outrageously different. We should not be hasty in our evaluation of patriarchs who encountered the assault of evil in life-and-death situations. At least they were engaged in the battle between fear and faith instead of hiding behind covert excuses for passivity and sloth as we often do.

I'm incapable of critiquing Abraham's theology. I don't know to what extent he was aware of his sinful nature, but his decisions regarding Sarah reveal dark moments in the life of an otherwise stalwart believer.

Not once, but twice Abraham hit the panic button and concocted a shady scheme of escape. Twice he wilted in fear rather than wait in faith. In both situations, once with Pharaoh and once with Abimelech, he behaved like a crafty coward rather than a valiant man of honor. Both times it was God's gracious intervention that made the strategic difference. When God plagued Pharaoh with debilitating diseases, it forced the return of

Sarah to Abraham. When God appeared to Abimelech in a dream and warned him of certain death, he quickly released Sarah. Twenty-five years separated Abraham's first ruse against Pharaoh and his later scam against Abimelech. Had Abraham learned anything about trusting God during two and a half decades? Did he forget the value of waiting upon God's perfect timing?

Something inside of me wants to rail at Abraham and consign him to public shaming. My indignation wanes, however, when I consider my absurd schemes of running ahead of God. So many of the tangled messes in my life have dots that connect to my refusal to wait and trust the Lord. I have learned the painful lesson that if I plant impatience in my heart, fertilize it with fear, and irrigate it with haste, I will reap the consequence of a rotten harvest.

While we may rightly contend that Abraham's appalling treatment of his wife was below the level of an amoeba, our outrage does not entitle us to presume that our sins and failures are negligible by comparison. Perhaps a wise conclusion can be drawn from the Irish playwright Oscar Wilde. He said, "The only difference between the saint and the sinner is that every saint has a past and every sinner has a future."[5]

Abraham's third crisis involved the snare of running ahead of God's promise. Waiting for brief periods can be annoying. But enduring a severe wait can be exhausting. It drains our resolve. It overloads the limit of our devotion. We ask ourselves if there is something in the fine print of God's plan that we got wrong. Abraham and Sarah may have asked the same question. Their golden years had turned brown with fatigue. The maternity clothes had been discarded, and the bassinette was forgotten. God had not fulfilled His promise to give them a son, and time was running out.

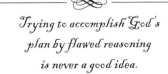

Trying to accomplish God's plan by flawed reasoning is never a good idea.

Consequently, they drew up a plan to bypass God's timing and accelerate their dream. They decided to solve the wait problem by helping God with a solution. Trying to accomplish God's plan by flawed reasoning is never a good idea. Our culture shares a common flaw with Abraham and Sarah. We are infected with the same "hurry sickness." We rush through our days, flustered by any and every delay. We scamper from one event to the next. We fuss about slow cars in express lanes, so we speed like drivers at a Nascar race trying to secure a pole position. We pant for more time in our day so that we can hurry to accomplish more things we desire. But even if we find ourselves with more time, why do we fill the extra minutes with more breathless haste? Moreover, why do we make impulsive decisions rather than pausing to slow down and soak up God's counsel?

Sarah knew how much Abraham wanted and needed a son. She knew her own barrenness. She knew that her servant Hagar could serve as a surrogate. It all seemed so logical and so accommodating. She may have wondered how could it be wrong if it felt so right. Especially since the culture and tradition approved of men fathering children with women who were not their wives.

At first, all the details fell smoothly into place. Everything worked according to plan. Sarah's recommendation plus Hagar's compliance equaled Abraham's delight. But the bitter consequences of running ahead of God began to surface. Disobedience can carry a harsh penalty. When Hagar conceived, she despised Sarah. In turn, Sarah mistreated Hagar and blamed Abraham. Abraham dodged accountability and told Sarah to deal with Hagar. This story reads like the script of a dysfunctional family in a disappointing novel.

Hagar gave birth to a son she named Ishmael in obedience to God's instruction. God assured her that Ishmael would have countless descendants. He also declared that Ishmael would become an unrestrained antagonist, "a wild donkey of a man."[6] Hardly the description that a young mother desires for her son. But the days morphed into years as Hagar, Abraham, and Sarah looked upon Ishmael as the heir of the future.

It's not a shocker that we grow accustomed to our preferences as time passes. We develop affection for the Ishmaels of our making. We convince ourselves that since our plan has worked so suitably then surely God approves. We settle for something far less than God's promise because we lack the discipline of holy grit. I have discovered that holy grit involves a crucifixion of my feet that race ahead of God's will and run away from God's direction.

Holy Grit endures a severe wait that leads to the death of selfish ambition. I have learned that it means clinging to God's promise when the only strength you have is one finger gripping

We settle for something far less than God's promise because we lack the discipline of holy grit.

His truth and barely enough stamina to hang on. But by His grace, you do. You continue to believe Him when your heart is bruised by doubt. You continue to follow Him when loneliness surrounds you and disappointment dogs you. Holy grit engages in a theatre of battle where the flesh wars against the spirit in ruthless assault, and you know that unless God intervenes, you will be completely overwhelmed. So you watch and wait and trust and obey.

After thirteen years with Ishmael at his side, Abraham had bonded with the son of his haste. Consequently, when God informed Abraham that Sarah would at long last give birth, Abraham begged God to allow Ishmael to be the blessed heir.[7]

How sadly ironic that at a moment when a severe wait was about to be rewarded with the fulfillment of God's promise, Abraham wished for Ishmael to be accepted as the appointed child. Abraham wanted his preferred plan so dearly that he urged God to jettison the divine plan. Like Abraham, we often find it heart-wrenching to part with the Ishmael of our desire, and we find it difficult to embrace the Isaac of God's will.

Unconditional Surrender

God reserves the right to test our faith at any time. I once was sure that my toughest battles would come early in my faith journey. I thought that by the time I reached middle age, all the trials and tests would be in my rearview mirror. After three decades of ministry, I imagined myself strolling through life celebrating spiritual victories and basking beneath blue skies of heavenly blessings.

After eleven decades, Abraham may have entertained a similar perspective. The wondering and wandering years seemed over. He and Sarah were soaking up the pleasure of Isaac and dancing in the delight of God's blessings. Everything was good. Very good. Until God interrupted the bliss with an ultimate test of unconditional surrender. Our English word "test" in Gen. 22:1 is translated from a Hebrew verb that points to proving the validity of something.[8] Whenever God tests us, He does it to prove to us the quality of our devotion. God knew what lay within Abraham. He knows what lies in you and me. The test is designed to prove to us the measure of our faith. The character of God is not on trial, but our character is.

In some way, big or small, every test contains vital lessons we can apply to our faith. Sometimes we fail miserably, to our embarrassment. Sometimes we pass admirably, to our amazement. Each test can point out a weakness or affirm a strength. I confess that some tests leave scars as a necessary mark of identification. Whenever I speak to pastors in a college or seminary class, I advise them to question a leader who bears no scars. The Lord is better served by the quiet and constant faith of a scarred follower than by the noisy and vain boast of a preening moralist.

David Livingstone's impact on Africa is incalculable. His unflinching determination to spread the gospel and end slavery speaks to my soul. He endured years of emotional isolation and physical deprivation for the renown of Christ. When he died, his heart was removed and buried beneath a tree in Chitambo's Village, Ilala, Africa. His body was dried, wrapped, and shipped to England. Months later, when his body arrived, his features were badly deteriorated. Many who admired Livingstone entertained doubts that the body was his. Skepticism invaded hope. Identification was verified, however, by the scarred and broken left shoulder that was mauled by a lion.[9] Scars can reveal wounds that have healed, but they also serve as tutors whose lessons are seldom cheap.

God gave Abraham a severe test that left scars of faith unmatched by other Old Testament characters. Abraham must have thought it horribly incomprehensible and so unlike God to require such a sacrifice. God's instruction dripped with pathos as Abraham heard Him say, "Take your son, your only son Isaac, whom you love, and go to the land of Moriah and offer him as a burnt offering."[10] In the Hebrew text, the verb "take" is followed by a two-letter Hebrew word "na" that is translated hundreds of times in the Old Testament to mean "now" or "please." Interestingly, that little word is used only five times when God addresses a person. Each time, it is connected with a request to do something so baffling that it seems unimaginable.[11]

When Abraham heard the details of God's test, he likely trembled. God was asking Abraham for the absolute relinquishment of Isaac. God was not tempting him to do what was wrong. God's faithful tenderness cushioned the harshness of the command.[12]

He was testing Abraham to do what was right by faith. God never withholds the pain of laying our Isaac on the altar.

I watched Reggie and Jenny Bostick lay their Isaac down in the sandy soil of a South Georgia cemetery. One Saturday night in August, they had fallen asleep anticipating joyful worship with friends the next day at church. Instead, they were awakened by a law enforcement official tenderly informing them that Cleve, their 22-year-old son, had been killed by a drunk driver. In an instant, their hearts were broken beyond repair. The pain of grief was more crippling than anything they had ever faced. Giant waves of sorrow crashed upon them. Cleve was in his senior year at the University of Georgia. He was planning to help his dad with farming after graduation. Family dreams of a flourishing future vanished instantly. Desperate questions surfaced as they would for anyone in a moment like that: Why God? Why did you allow our son to die like this? How can we possibly hear your voice in the midst of our worst nightmare?

Reggie and Jenny held tightly to each other and enveloped their daughter Kiley. I wept with them and found it hard to maintain my composure on the day of Cleve's funeral. My mind raced with memories. Sweet images of Cleve as a toddler with chubby arms around his mother's neck. Cleve as a third grader dressed in camo, ready to go hunting with his dad. Cleve as a brother who delighted to hang around his sister Kiley when they were both students cheering for the Georgia Bulldogs.

The small Baptist church, appropriately named Hopeful, was packed with students and friends. Many stood around the walls and in the foyer. Everyone felt the heavy sorrow, but Reggie and Jenny modeled absolute surrender. And I saw holy grit defined in raw authenticity.

When I think of that beloved couple, I think about a severe wait connected to the Apostle Paul's statement, "For I consider that

> *We don't get to set the price tag on obedience. But we do have the opportunity to trust God ever how expensive the sacrifice.*

the sufferings of this present time are not worth comparing with the glory that is to be revealed to us. For the creation waits with eager longing for the revealing of the sons of God." (Rom. 8:18-19) ESV

As Abraham and Isaac meandered up the craggy slope of Moriah, they stopped to build an altar for worship. This is the first time that "worship" occurs in the Bible. Moriah was the place where hundreds of years later David asked to buy a threshing floor from Ornan to build an altar. When Ornan offered to give it rather than require a payment, David replied, "No, I will not offer a sacrifice to God that costs me nothing."[13]

I find it convincing that worship was initially expressed in a context of costly surrender. We don't get to set the price tags on obedience, but we do have the opportunity to trust God, ever how expensive the sacrifice. The voice of easy-button faith appeals to our flesh. We prefer shortcuts to holy grit without the heartbreak of sacrifice. God's plan for shaping us never bypasses the crucible of perseverance. I have tried to imagine the turmoil inside of Abraham. I have wondered about the compliance of Isaac. The entire situation strains my heart. It baffles my mind. How could Abraham surrender his deep love for his son? How could he forsake the covenant that Isaac represented? Why would God push Abraham to the edge of insanity?

From a human point of view, God's command made no sense. The radicality seemed appalling. There was nothing logical about it. After decades of waiting, Abraham was asked to relinquish the promise that confirmed his faith in God. But faith has its reasons that reason can't always comprehend. It's erroneous to think that God will never put more on you than you can handle. He will, however, never put more on you than He can handle. A crisis of faith can only be resolved by an unmitigated trust in God's purpose. Abraham didn't know how God would fulfill His promise to make a great nation through Isaac. Nevertheless, he intended to trust God's plan even if it meant eliminating God's promise. Abraham arrived at a gritty point where he was willing to give back to God what belonged to God from the start. He believed that God would somehow provide a solution. He believed that God was able to resurrect Isaac from death.[14] The undeniable mark of a godly person is an unflinching will to persevere. Abraham proved that his security did not lie with Isaac, but with God.

In his classic, *The Screwtape Letters*, C. S. Lewis illustrates the power of obedient faith. Screwtape, the elder demon, warns his nephew Wormwood about a Christian who follows God's will in the darkest moments, "Do not be deceived,

We prefer shortcuts to holy grit without the heartbreak of sacrifice. God's system of shaping us never bypasses the crucible of perseverance.

Wormwood. Our course is never more in danger than when a human, no longer desiring but still intending to do our Enemy's will, looks round upon a universe from which every trace of Him seems to have vanished, and asks why he has been forsaken and still obeys."[15] Those last three words "and still obeys" bleed holy grit. If you're like me, you prefer instant spiritual maturity without the trauma of suffering.

But the obedience God desires does not come with an easy button. His system for growing us into giant sequoias of holiness involves a relentless determination to "obey anyway" regardless of the circumstances. As Abraham tightened his grip on the knife, ready to sacrifice Isaac, God intervened with a thundering prohibition and provided a substitute for the sacrifice.

That moment and that place overwhelmed Abraham so supremely that he named it "God will provide."[16] Furthermore, the experience foreshadowed a future moment when God would provide the ultimate atonement for sin through His Son, our Savior, the perfect "Lamb of God who takes away the sin of the world."[17]

God grants extravagant blessings to those who honor Him with holy grit. His reward is infinitely greater than the cost of our surrender. Consequently, Abraham received the pleasure of God who declared, "In your seed, all the nations of the earth shall be blessed because you have obeyed my voice."[18] Abraham was able to obey because he believed that God could not and would not be unfaithful to Himself.

Abraham developed a gigantic capacity to wait on God. What's the size of your "wait" capacity? If you took a coffee cup to the ocean and filled it up, you would have a cup full. It's not that the ocean can't give you more. It's that your cup can't hold more. Your capacity will determine what you receive. In a similar way, our capacity to wait on God will affect what we receive from Him.

No wonder Abraham was called "the friend of God."[19] He endured a severe wait so holy and intimate that he was willing to offer his most treasured possession to God with the full assurance that God would guard whatever was given for His glory. We can be encouraged that the Lord takes all the details of our agony and affliction and writes a grace-saturated narrative about an eternal "weight" of glory. Sometimes this includes a severe "wait" for His glory. All the temptations we endure, all the sorrows and sufferings we face will pale in comparison to the incomparable splendor of eternity with Him. So we tarry with passionate anticipation. We wait expectantly with holy grit.

Gritty Take Aways

- **Wait faithfully upon God and pray for the will to persevere.** A severe wait will expose every flaw and fracture in your character. It will strain every fiber of your faith. We find it so exhausting because we have grown accustomed to immediate answers at the click of a mouse, fast food at the push of a button, and urgent entertainment at the tap of a screen.

- **Realize that God designs "what" you go through, but He allows you to decide "how" you go through it.** We all wait, but how we wait reflects our faith. Like Abraham, we sometimes take detours into Egypt because we decide God's pace is too slow. Detours contrary to God's direction lead us down paths of moral compromise. Holy grit, however, applies the wrench of God's power to the rusty bolt of unbelief and holds tightly until God turns obstacles of despair into opportunities for praise.

- **Trust the Lord to edit the ugly and confusing scripts you write.** He can shape them into a beautiful story for His glory. If we stare at one of Abraham's disgraceful chapters and disregard his other chapters of faith, then we will miss the compelling plot that the Lord developed from the choices he made and the risks he took. When we intend to write our life story as a narrative of obedience but find the pages blotted and marked by sin, God is able to edit everything for our growth and His glory.

CHAPTER 2

*To be a Christian means to forgive
the inexcusable, because God has
forgiven the inexcusable in you.*

C. S. Lewis

*Be on your guard; if your brother sins
rebuke him and if he repents forgive him.
If he sins against you seven times in a
day and comes back to you seven times
saying 'I repent' you must forgive him.*

Luke 17:3-CSB

*Forgiveness is not an occasional
act. It is a permanent attitude.*

Martin Luther King, Jr.

Joseph: Finding a Way to Forgive

Several days before Cardinal Joseph Ratzinger became the 265th Pope of the Roman Catholic Church, the Vatican faced a serious web dilemma. The domain name of "Benedict XVI.com" had already been bought and secured by Rogers Cadenhead. The impasse was broken when Cadenhead asked for an exchange. He wanted the Vatican to grant him the blessing of "complete absolution, no questions asked, for the third week of March, 1987."[1]

Can you identify with him? All of us have moments, if not weeks, that sear our memory and cry out for forgiveness. We are wired to need forgiveness whether or not we give or receive it. Medical authorities have long championed the benefit of forgiveness. Dr. Amit Sood,world renowned sprcialist in resilience and well-being and former professor of medicine at Mayo Clinic, points out that unforgiveness takes a serious toll on our health and suffocates us emotionally.[2]

If unforgiveness is so detrimental and forgiveness is so beneficial, why do we find it so hard to forgive? Why does it require a ton of holy grit?

One of the main reasons we struggle with forgiveness is that we misunderstand it.

- *Forgiveness is not condoning an offense. It does not require us to pretend that the pain and suffering didn't matter. Biblical forgiveness is neither wrapped in deception as if the transgression didn't occur nor covered in denial as if the injury didn't hurt.*
- *Forgiveness is not a magic wand we wave over an offender to guarantee repentance and behavioral transformation. It is not a trick to manipulate change in someone else. It is a*

posture of obedience to Christ. We can offer forgiveness, but the other person's behavior may never change. We can't coerce a favorable response.

- *Forgiveness is not a compromise of justice. God is not unjust. He knows the whole story. He judges without partiality. Evil will not prevail. God's justice ensures that terrorists will not get away with murder, and sex traffickers will not get away with unfathomable abuse.*

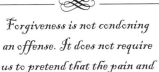

Forgiveness is not condoning an offense. It does not require us to pretend that the pain and suffering didn't matter.

- *Forgiveness is not synonymous with forgetting. Some wounds lodge so deep in the memory that they cannot be erased.*

The parents of the Amish children who were murdered by a deranged gunman will never forget the atrocity. Nevertheless, they demonstrated Christ-like forgiveness to the perpetrator's family and proved to the world that forgiving is not a casual dismissal of a crime, but a choice not to live enslaved in the memory of a profound tragedy. The parent's offer of forgiveness could not change the past, but it could alter the future. Forgiveness is less about forgetting and more about replacing hurt with grace so that our remembering is void of retaliation and malice. As followers of Christ, we can't afford to hold the poison of unforgiveness. We have been too excessively forgiven by Christ to withhold offering forgiveness to others. Forgiveness is central to the redemptive message of the Bible. It is so central that we can state with absolute conviction that there is no salvation without forgiveness. The reason forgiveness holds such a prominent place in Scripture is because we can never enjoy a right relationship with God unless we meet His conditions on His terms. Forgiveness originates with God. It was His purpose to apply grace to our sin without compromising His opposition to sin. Consequently, God's forgiveness was not cheap, easy, or simple. At the cross, He demonstrated the greatest forgiveness there ever was and ever will be. At the cross, Jesus fulfilled Isaiah's prophesy: "He was pierced for our transgressions, and He was crushed for our iniquities. Upon Him was the chastisement that brought us peace, and with His wounds we are healed."[3]

It is crucial to note that God's forgiveness involves both provision and appropriation. We appropriate what He provides when we receive what He offers. We experience His forgiveness when we repent of our sins and trust what His Son accomplished on our behalf. Consequently, the forgiveness we embrace through Jesus is the foundation of the forgiveness we can offer to others. I am convinced that believers who live closest to Jesus can swim through the deep waters of forgiveness because they know that nursing the wounds they received are inconsequential compared to the forgiveness that Jesus paid by His wounds. Forgiving others flows out of the forgiveness we have experienced in Christ.

Writing this chapter compelled me to revisit a painful memory of a church conflict. My wife and I had poured our love and leadership into a church where we imagined we would spend the rest of our lives ministering. During those fourteen years, our children graduated from high school and college, discovered godly soul mates, and celebrated marriage. The church experienced phenomenal growth and became one of the first churches in our state to develop a multi-site campus. God graciously used me to lead the congregation through several transitions, including a couple of major multi-million dollar building campaigns as the membership swelled to nearly 6,000. Hundreds of lives were being impacted by the gospel each year. We thought the years ahead would be equally as rewarding. But a spirit of rancor and divisiveness slithered into the staff and a small group of members.

As a veteran leader, I should have expected the unexpected. I knew that all problems were not spiritual problems, but I should have paid more attention to the spiritual warfare that was stirring. I knew that the Adversary could turn friends into foes and differences into disasters. Sadly, I was unable to stop the escalation of an unnecessary controversy into an unwarranted conflict. It was an issue that never should have gathered momentum, but it developed into a perfect storm.

Forgiveness is less about forgetting and more about replacing hurt with grace so that our remembering is void of retaliation and malice.

A gale of bewilderment swept over my soul. I felt that I had failed to safely guide the congregation through a crisis. My wife and I grieved and prayed for an amicable resolution to the discord. After several weary months, we asked God to allow us to leave. Taking the high road can involve a crucified choice. The painful process of forgiveness can mean making yourself of no reputation and permitting the critics to hammer the nails into your ministry.

Resigning was sweet torture. Sweet because Jesus' presence overwhelmed us with tender assurance. Torture because we felt rootless. We had been embedded in the soil of a community we treasured. Leaving friends who did not understand our decision seemed to them like an alienation of affection. It's risky trying to comprehend God's purpose in seasons of hurt even if we know that "behind a frowning providence He hides a smiling face."[4] What we couldn't realize during that travail was that God was orchestrating something far more amazing than anything we could have imagined. The vital lessons He would teach us about forgiveness were priceless.

A Pit of Family Abuse

The morning that Joseph obeyed his father and set out to locate his brothers carried no hint of God's intended purpose. At seventeen, Joseph was learning the family trade of shepherding. His family, however, was a melting pot of strife and discord that simmered with rivalry, rage, and lust.

Joseph was the firstborn son of Rachel and Jacob. He was a sibling in a mixed family representing four different mothers. His brothers perceived him as the favorite of their father, Jacob. In a grand display of affection, Jacob bestowed upon Joseph a luxurious colorful robe symbolic of a privileged position. Such extravagant partiality did not go unnoticed by his brothers. They "hated" him so much they could not speak a kind word to him.[5] The Hebrew term for their hatred denotes an intense animosity.[6] While Joseph's brothers bore responsibility for their animus, Joseph's father bore responsibility for his favoritism.

Roland Warren, former President of the National Fatherhood Initiative, emphasized that Jacob made several "bad dad" mistakes, but his primary error was turning a blind eye to sibling rivalry.[7]

Research regarding parental favoritism reveals a disturbing pattern of conflict between siblings. Clinical studies indicate that the effects of parental favoritism upon children wield a detrimental impact upon siblings long after childhood and well into adulthood.[8]

When Joseph told his brothers about a dream in which he saw them bowing down to him, it was hardly the first instance of rivalry. Joseph's motivation for sharing his dream was not revealed. Perhaps it arose from a youthful impulse to communicate an amazing revelation he had received. Perhaps it was spoken with a condescending tone in an attempt to even a score with his brothers. Whatever the reason, Joseph's brothers' attitude continued to harden against him. His dreams would later be proven true, but on the day he traveled to Dothan, his brothers were ready to end his dreams.

Sometimes close friends or those in your own family can become your worst nightmare. They can abuse you emotionally and physically. They can shame you with ridicule. They can sabotage your noble dreams and feel no hesitation about disposing of you in a pit. Sadly, they can barter your worth to cheap traffickers.

Joseph's brothers saw him coming and devised a lethal plan.[9] Reuben, the oldest brother, seemed to be the only one with a conscience. He objected to the idea of murder and proposed an alternate plan in hope of later rescuing Joseph. Regardless of his good intentions, Reuben's plan to assuage abuse by moderation completely failed. It usually does. During a moment of evil, discreet timidity is seldom able to prevent a harmful outcome.

The brothers stripped Joseph of his coat. They threw him with all his dreams into the bottom of a dry well. Then they calmly "sat down to eat a meal."[10] What depth of malice does that statement reveal? How much do you have to hate someone to plot a murder, cast him into a pit, then blithely ignore his plight by wolfing down a cheese sandwich?

An approaching caravan of Ishmaelite traders en route to Egypt not only interrupted the brothers' meal but provided a plan to sell Joseph. In a matter of minutes, he became a slave. Did Joseph stare at his brothers in disbelief as he was hustled away?

Later the brothers casually soaked Joseph's luxurious coat with the blood of a slaughtered goat. They took it back to their father. Can you picture the scene? They pull back the entrance flap of Jacob's tent and throw the bloodied coat on the floor. Jacob glances at it and then studies the harsh expression of his sons. "We found this," they exclaim with feigned sincerity. "Does it belong to your son?" they ask. Jacob wondered why they said "your son" instead of "our brother." He gently takes the coat and fingers the familiar colors of the weave. He knows it belongs to Joseph. His voice chokes with grief. He concludes that a wild beast has killed Joseph. He moans painfully. Jacob, the man who wrestled with God's messenger and prevailed, falls down in the dirt of his tent, pinned beneath inconsolable anguish. The sins of his past revisit him through the wickedness of his sons. As Jacob deceived his father with the skin of an animal, so his sons now deceive him with the blood of an animal. Joseph was considered dead. Jacob's world was changed.

And somewhere in the sands of Sinai, a forsaken and abused teenager shuffled toward Egypt chained to a caravan of slave traders, but guided by God's sovereignty.

Undeserved Wounds

Joseph didn't deserve the trauma of abuse and abandonment. He didn't deserve the indignity and hostile treatment of being sold as a slave and removed hundreds of miles from home. Nobody does.

God enables holy grit to develop at a divine pace in the oven of perseverance rather than in the microwave of impulse.

If bitterness needed a foot in the door of Joseph's life, he had a reason to kick it wide open. His mind swirled with questions for which he had no answers. However, God was preparing him for a day when he would have answers that he no longer questioned. What seemed at the time to be the end of a good life as he knew it would become a better life like he had never known. But not quickly. God enables holy grit to develop at a divine pace in the oven of perseverance rather than in the microwave of impulse.

Life in Egypt became Joseph's new reality. Surrounded by people speaking a language he didn't understand, in a culture he didn't comprehend, he accepted his role under Potiphar's authority. Potiphar held the title of captain in Pharaoh's guard. The Hebrew word meaning "guard" can refer to someone who slaughtered animals as well as someone who executed prisoners. Could Potiphar have been an executioner?[11] His job may have included supervision of the execution of criminals guilty of capital offenses against Pharaoh. Potiphar was not the man a slave wanted to defy. So Joseph went to work for a tough, unbelieving boss in a place where the fruit of humility and accountability would grow best.

Alone in Egypt, the odds stood against a bright and promising future. Joseph had been discarded like a dirty napkin by his brothers. He found himself meeting the demands of a pagan employer in an idol-worshipping culture. He felt erased, totally forgotten, except for five words of affirmation that turned futility into doxology: "The Lord was with Joseph."[12] The Lord was with Joseph to heal the wounds of rejection and worthlessness that threatened to destroy him. All Joseph had was God. Is that enough? Is God enough when despair mocks the slender thread of faith you hold? Is He enough when failure crushes your dreams? When shame devours your hope? Joseph owned nothing. But God owned Joseph. God is always enough when you are totally His. When you are owned by God, others observe your character. They notice your temperament under stress. They watch how you treat others around you. Potiphar noticed that God was with Joseph. He put Joseph in charge of his entire estate and made him the chief operating officer. Potiphar didn't have faith in God like Joseph, but he recognized the faith that such a man practiced. He took delight in Joseph and enjoyed having him around the house. So did Mrs. Potiphar, but for different reasons. She studied

Joseph's handsome face, and her eyes followed him with seductive interest. She entertained lustful thoughts. Her fantasies gave way to action as she invited Joseph to sleep with her.

Few slaves in Joseph's sandals would have resisted such a proposal. After all, slaves were obligated to meet any demand of their owners. Joseph felt the sway of temptation. He withstood the attraction because his desire to obey God was stronger than the opportunity to satisfy temporary pleasure. His devotion to God took precedence over a sexual impulse. Some temptations strike immediately and pass quickly. The one facing Joseph continued day after day. The most difficult temptations to repel are the relentless ones. The protracted appeal. The persistent offer. The unceasing pressure.

Deepwater explorers are keenly aware of pressure. Engineer Jacques Piccard and U. S. Navy Lt. Don Walsh became the first individuals to reach the deepest place in the Earth's ocean. They descended 35,800 feet into the Mariana Trench SW of Guam in the Pacific Ocean.

To put that into perspective, it is one mile deeper than Mount Everest is high. The excessive pressure of 16,000 lbs. per square inch upon their submersible named the Trieste required a five-inch-thick metal wall around the sphere in which Piccard and Walsh sat. On their journey to the bottom, they passed several species of fish that were unaffected by the pressure. The fish moved and whirled with ease under a force that would instantly crush an unprotected human. How can we account for the startling difference? God designed the fish to thrive because the pressure within them is equal to the pressure on the outside. Similarly, God's dominance in Joseph's life was equal to but resistant to the temptation from Mrs. Potiphar. Nevertheless, she continued her subtle strategy. One day when Joseph was working in the house and the other servants were not, she grabbed his garment and insisted that he have sex with her. Joseph turned away. She held him tightly, but he fled, leaving his garment in her hands. For the second time in his young life, Joseph lost a garment. Mrs. Potiphar fabricated a story for her husband. To cover her ploy, she falsely accused Joseph and enticed Potiphar to throw him in prison. Once again Joseph became a castaway, and the undeserved wounds continued to accumulate.

I have a friend who is a wound care specialist. He helps patients who suffer from chronic wounds by removing necrotic tissue through a procedure called debridement. "When the dead tissue is allowed to remain it hinders the development of healthy new tissue and makes the wound more susceptible to infection. Debriding is often the best step toward healing," he claims. Healing the wounds we don't deserve requires a sacred surgery. A cutting away of the residual deadness that hinders healthy recovery. Every wounding crisis in Joseph's life found a transformation through the scalpel of God's sovereignty.

God allowed Joseph to be wounded. God doesn't plan evil, but He has a plan to use evil for our good and His glory. Prison became a university of adversity where God cut away the septic need for retaliation. Moreover, Joseph's incarceration served as a hidden doorway that ushered him into Pharaoh's inner circle. Can we identify with Joseph? Our spiritual myopia often hinders our perspective on God's long-term plan. We strain to see how God sows the seed of spiritual maturity in our suffering. Yet, it is our wounds that compel us to need His presence.

Healing the wounds we don't deserve requires a sacred surgery. A cutting away of residual deadness that hinders healthy recovery.

Mark Buchanan wisely wrote, "Wounds are, in Christ's

economy, a means of God's wooing. It is the strange kiss of God, the reverse of the Judas kiss – a kiss to restore us and not to betray us. The pain becomes a narrow passage that leads down into a unique intimacy with the suffering servant." [13]

God gave Joseph discernment in the squalor of a prison as he learned to interpret dreams. He accurately explained the dreams of a baker and a cup-bearer and how one would die and the other would be restored to his position with Pharaoh.

Two years later, when Pharaoh needed someone to explain his dreams, the cup-bearer recommended Joseph. Pharaoh listened to Joseph's disclaimer that he could not interpret a dream by himself. He could only do it by God's enabling. He explained that God would grant seven years of economic abundance followed by seven years of severe famine. To prepare for the hard years of poverty, Joseph suggested that Pharaoh appoint an intelligent and wise leader who could organize and implement a survival plan. Pharaoh saw strategic leadership qualities in Joseph and appointed him to wield authority over all of Egypt. The fingerprints of God marked Joseph's story. At seventeen years of age, he entered Egypt as a lonely nobody. At thirty, he was second in command over a great nation. Only God could take someone that nobody values and value that person like nobody could.

Releasing Our Abusers

God places and displaces us for reasons we don't always understand. He elevated Joseph beyond all expectations. Joseph's brothers had banished him into a dark hole. But God made him second only to Pharaoh. His brothers tore the beautiful robe off Joseph's back. God used Pharaoh to give him the finest clothes in Egypt. His brothers decided he was worthless. God proved that Joseph was treasured.

Over two decades had passed since he was purchased as a slave. He exercised leadership wisely as the "vizier," the prime minister at the head of an administrative bureaucracy.[14] He successfully supervised food storage in all the cities of Egypt. He was a loving husband to Asenath and a proud father to Manasseh and Ephraim. His sons bore names associated with his past affliction. Manasseh's name meant "forgetful." Ephraim's name meant "fruitful." God equipped him to disregard the former trauma and to focus on the present blessings.

Joseph stood upon the summit of success. He had no reason to look back. He felt no need to rehearse the abuse in his past. Sometimes, however, the past meets us when we least expect it. Half-healed wounds can continue to ooze. They leak at random moments when a painful memory returns.

To be unforgiving is to take a one-way ride into the black hole of malice. To be unforgiven is to endure a slow bleed toward a pitiless death.

Seeping wounds of the soul resist healing when the poisons of doubt and disillusion spread. Doubt because you thought you had moved beyond the hurt. Disillusion because you wonder if you will ever be able to forgive freely. Yet living unforgiven and being unforgiving are mutually destructive. To be "unforgiving" is to take a one-way ride into the black hole of malice. To be "unforgiven" is to endure a slow bleed toward a pitiless death.

When Joseph's brothers arrived to buy grain, forgiveness was not on their minds or his. But it was on God's heart. God receives the glory when we accept forgiveness. Moreover, we find liberation when we practice it.

Indeed, it is hard for us to read God's autograph on the pages of our tears. Harder still when He writes a script that forces us to face betrayal, slander, injury, and injustice. Perhaps hardest when he asks us to fill unforgivable moments with unbridled mercy toward our offenders.

Joseph recognized his brothers. Did the tone of their voice grab his attention? Was it the peculiarity of their Hebrew accent? Their attire? In that nanosecond of recognition, did Joseph feel a rush for payback? Four times he accused his brothers of spying.[15] They emphatically denied it. They explained that they were all sons of one father, but one brother had stayed home with their father. They mentioned another brother who was no longer living. He was dead. Erased. Gone. To them, Joseph didn't matter. To Joseph, the matter had to be settled. He threw the brothers in prison for three days and released them under one stipulation. They could take their grain back to their families, but they had to bring back Benjamin, their youngest brother, while Simeon remained in prison.

If this were a revenge scene in a Hollywood movie, we might expect to hear a menacing soundtrack as Joseph meets his brothers. Imagine the action like this: Joseph wipes the sweat from his brow and turns to hear a faintly familiar voice. He listens. He studies ten bearded men asking a clerk for several hundred pounds of grain. The sight of their profile and the sound of their inflection stirred an awakening. Suddenly in an "aha" moment, Joseph recognizes them. The buried pages in a hidden book of pain come alive again. His heart races. His anger rises. The men cannot miss the scornful stare from Joseph. They watch his fingers form into fists as the muscles in his forearms bulge and twitch. Joseph walks closer and speaks firmly through a translator. "So you need grain? Is that right?" He paces methodically and circles around them. His voice gets louder. "You are filthy spies disguised as merchants! You would like nothing more than to exploit a weakness in Pharaoh's land." Reuben, the oldest, retorts, "No, sir. We are. . ." "Silence!" Joseph demands. Slowly he continues his monologue in a mocking tone. "I know a man who once knew you! He was nothing more than someone you despised and sold like a cheap piece of property. He said you broke something inside of him that never healed. He claimed that as months became years, the question of "why" haunted his soul and begged for an answer. Do you have an answer I may give him?"

Joseph places his hand on Judah's shoulder and stares into his eyes. "So now you want grain? Did you ever consider what was needed when that man begged you not to harm him? So, you and your children are hungry? When you were enjoying lamb chops and lentils and sipping your wine, did you ever wonder what happened to him?" The men grow wide-eyed with fear when Joseph adds, "Did you ever feel a hint of remorse for selling him to a caravan of slave traders?"

Joseph raises his voice to a crescendo. "For three days I'm going to keep you in prison. I will then release you. The only way you can prove you are not spies is for one of you to remain in prison."

Half-healed wounds can continue to ooze. They leak at random moments when a painful memory returns.

The rest of you must go home and bring your youngest brother back." "Leave now," he thunders, "before I unleash the wrath of Pharaoh upon you. Perhaps the wolves of Palestine will devour your flesh so your father won't have to look any longer at the vermin he raised as sons." Thankfully, the biblical narrative about Joseph is not a movie scene laced with scorching vitriol. It's a miracle scene that drips with firm truth and extravagant forgiveness.

So, what was Joseph's strategy of forgiveness? How did he find a way to forgive? First, Joseph responded courageously to a divine appointment. When Joseph first recognized his brothers, he had several choices. He could pretend they didn't harm him badly and "trivialize" their sin. He could excuse their wrongdoing and "rationalize" their sin. He could explode in rage and "brutalize" his brothers for their sin. Best, however, Joseph could trust God and exercise courage to confront them about their sin. God arranged the opportunity for him to forgive his brothers, and Joseph seized the moment. God faithfully provides occasions for believers to practice forgiveness today. Our response must be one of courageous obedience. Giving and receiving forgiveness is not for wimps!

Second, Joseph discerned forgiveness by testing his brothers' willingness to receive it. For example, suppose a friend takes your car and you find it in his driveway a mile away. You call and meet with him to ask why he took it without your consent. If he adamantly replies, "I don't have to answer to you, Bozo and I didn't do anything wrong," then you know he's not wringing his hands waiting to be forgiven. Testing someone's willingness to receive forgiveness requires godly wisdom to accomplish a godly goal. It should never be exercised with prideful legalism. Joseph cleverly planned a way to get all his brothers to meet with him and hopefully heal a deep ache.

He began with a firm demand that they bring Benjamin to him. It effectively awakened their dormant conscience. They discussed the matter among themselves and felt the sting of guilt. They admitted their contempt toward Joseph when they shoved him down a well. They sensed the punishment of God.

The brothers finally persuaded their father, Jacob, to allow Benjamin to return with them to Egypt. After their arrival, Joseph planned a meeting around a banquet table. Was it coincidental that he assigned seating for them in order from the oldest to the youngest? Apologist Henry Morris claims that this was hardly an accident because there were "39,917,000" different orders in which eleven individuals could have been seated. The odds were nearly "forty million to one against it."[16] Furthermore, the seating assignments astonished the brothers and compelled them to realize that the Prince of Egypt knew something alarmingly well.

An argument can be made that "testing" someone's willingness to be forgiven is inappropriate. After all, shouldn't it be offered automatically and unconditionally? Perhaps, but not so fast. There is a personal benefit when we offer forgiveness. We cease to be hostage to our fear and anger. Furthermore, the freedom from bitterness can be exhilarating. But we must not confuse forgiveness with altruism. If forgiveness is understood merely as a therapeutic pain reliever, it loses its theological significance. When forgiveness serves only as an emotional analgesic, it too easily becomes a substitutionary opioid numbing the gravity of an offense and pacifying an offender. Biblical forgiveness never minimizes the pain of injustice for the sole purpose of feeling better. The core question about forgiveness is this: Should we practice it like our Heavenly Father and apply it as He instructed us in Scripture? He offers forgiveness to all, but He places a condition upon it for anyone who receives it. He states that we must confess our wrongdoing and place our faith in Him for the cancellation of our transgression. When we approach Him with repentance and confession of sin, He is faithful and just to forgive us and to cleanse us from all unrighteousness.[17]

God's "disposition" of forgiveness is consistently tilted toward those who wrong Him. The "transaction" of forgiveness occurs, however, only when a favorable response is made to His conditions. For

Biblical forgiveness never minimizes the pain of an injustice for the sole purpose of feeling better.

us to practice forgiving others, we must maintain a disposition of forgiveness toward them. Hands extended. Hearts open. The effective transaction of forgiveness is satisfied when it is humbly received by the wrongdoer. This transaction should not be considered meritorious work on behalf of the offender. If I wrong someone and seek forgiveness, I am not earning forgiveness. If I receive forgiveness, it is not because of my worthiness but because of the forgiver's grace. John Stott explained it like this: "To forgive and to ask forgiveness are both costly exercises. All authentic Christian peace-making exhibits the love and justice – and so the pain – of the cross."[18] God's forgiveness comes to us dripping with grace at the cost of His Son who satisfied the perfection of the Father's justice. It is transacted when we repent of our sin and place our faith in Him. Similarly, Joseph's forgiveness strategy was simple: to help his brothers realize their need for repentance by testing their willingness to be forgiven.

A Feast of Forgiveness

Byron Hollinshead asked a team of superb historians about scenes in history they wish they could have witnessed. All the responses focused on crucial moments that served as turning points for humanity. Scenes like John Quincy Adams contending for liberty in the trial of the Amistad and the blissfully unaware Abraham Lincoln on the day he was assassinated, planning a trip with his wife for an enjoyable evening at Ford's Theater.[19]

I'm not an esteemed historian, but I wish I could have been present when Joseph stunned his brothers by revealing his identity and offering them forgiveness. I wish I could have seen their dejected countenance as they stared at the floor, huddled before Joseph, who held the authority to imprison and execute them. I wish I could have seen Joseph unleashing his raw, pent-up passion.

When he reached an emotional peak with his brothers, he erupted. He wailed so loudly that Pharaoh's household heard it. Then gathering his voice, he firmly declared, "I am Joseph." His brothers were so shocked they couldn't respond. Panic paralyzed them. Their one dominant thought centered on what would happen next. Revenge seemed probable, but forgiveness was not on their radar. Grace must have been the furthest thing from their imagination.

Astonishingly, Joseph modeled the holy grit of forgiveness in several ways. First, he invited his brothers to draw near to him. It's difficult to determine vocal tone from a written text, but the context implies an empathetic and wooing quality in Joseph's plea. Forgiveness breathes best in an atmosphere of proximity. Relational distance increases misunderstanding, but nearness enhances communication and trust. Trust seemed to grow in Joseph's heart sequentially from the first encounter when he overheard his brothers express their guilt until the crowning moment when Judah offered himself as a substitute for Benjamin. Trust serves as the mortar for repairing broken relationships.

Second, Joseph spoke truth wrapped in kindness. He revealed that he was their brother, and he also pointed out that they had "sold him." Forgiveness never hides behind a façade of pretense. It upholds honesty and accuracy. Joseph clearly stated the offense his brothers had committed, but he framed it with gentleness and concern.

Third, he could offer forgiveness because he chose to view his wounds through the prism of God's purpose. Four times Joseph emphasized to his brothers that God was at work through all his troubles.[20] God always fulfills His promise. If I make you a promise, I will do my best to honor it, but I know that I could fail you. My best resolve could dissolve because of my human inability or because of my sinful capability.

God never fails, however. He never blunders. He never fumbles a single detail as He crafts His purpose to achieve His promise. God worked faithfully in every facet of Joseph's life to fulfill His covenant promise. For this reason, Joseph could say to his brothers, "You planned evil against me, but God planned it for good to bring about the present result, the survival of many people."[21] Joseph wasn't dismissing their abuse, betrayal, and greed. He called his brothers' deeds evil. Nevertheless, he left the ultimate judgment with God. Joseph believed God's purpose carried inherent goodness that could not only conquer evil but could conform it to accomplish a holy result – the "survival of many people" and the continuation of the Hebrew lineage. Joseph relied upon God during all his painful weary years. He learned to lean hard into God. When we see our wounds as part of God's weaving and see our disappointments as His appointments, we can discover our significance in His refining intent. We can extend forgiveness freely to others even if they are as shocked by our offer as Joseph's brothers were by his.

Fourth, Joseph modeled forgiveness because he refused to nurse a grudge. The fountain of God's grace washed from Joseph any desire to seek revenge.

A grudge is nothing less than bitterness aged in a keg of hatred. It is toxic. Whenever there is a large oil spill in the ocean, like the BP Deepwater Horizon accident or the Exxon Valdez crash, sludge creeps into rocky inlets and coastal estuaries, covering marine life and birds. The oily muck of sludge carries death. A grudge is sludge that poisons a relationship. A grudge suffocates. Forgiveness liberates. A grudge destroys.

> *A grudge is sludge that poisons a relationship. A grudge suffocates. Forgiveness liberates. A grudge destroys. Forgiveness restores. A grudge demeans. Forgiveness edifies.*

Forgiveness restores. A grudge demeans. Forgiveness edifies. A grudge feeds at the table of contempt and spite. Forgiveness dines at a feast of grace and hope.

Finding a way to forgive can sometimes seem impossible. Hetty was an intelligent and beautiful follower of Christ. She learned Latin and Greek as a child growing up in a pastor's home. She was the daughter of Samuel Wesley, and the sister of John Wesley, the founder of the Methodist movement in England. Her other brother, Charles wrote hundreds of poems that later became lyrics for Christian hymns. Hetty was equally as gifted and passionate in faith as her brothers. By the time she was twenty-five, she fell deeply in love with a school teacher who assisted her father, Samuel. On the occasion of a visit to her home, the school teacher sang a song that annoyed Samuel, who promptly told him to leave and never return. Her father's harsh legalism wounded Hetty. She was devastated. Her mother tried to intervene, but Samuel refused to listen. He sent Hetty out of town to care for an elderly couple who lived miles away.

As the months passed, Hetty became lonely, miserable, and careless about the future. She yielded to temptation and became pregnant. Her only recourse was a return home where her father locked her in a room giving her a diet of bread and water. He would show her no mercy. Samuel quickly forced her into marriage but refused to perform the ceremony himself. Hetty's husband was a churlish man who spent most of his evenings at a pub and returned home drunk. Hetty gave birth to a baby girl, but the child died a few months later.

Hetty desperately wanted her father's forgiveness. She returned home seeking it a few years later, but he would not allow her to enter.[22] John felt deep sympathy for his sister and preached a sermon about forgiving those who repent. Her father heard it and took offense at John. Samuel Wesley died without offering the one thing his daughter needed most. Fifteen years passed until Hetty died. A profound sadness followed her to the grave. There is no evidence that she received the forgiveness that she craved the most from her father.[23]

Hopefully, the person you need to forgive has not hurt you in the same way Hetty Wesley was hurt. But is Jesus bringing someone to mind as you read these lines? Let me encourage you not to rush past these uncomfortable questions. Linger here. Ask the Lord to search your thoughts.

Is there someone to whom you should offer forgiveness?

- A work associate who lied about you?
- A friend who slandered your family's reputation?
- A professor who mocked you?
- A parent who abused you verbally?
- A relative who abused you sexually?

Is there someone from whom you should seek forgiveness?

- Someone you hurt a long time ago?
- A sibling you ridiculed or spurned recently?
- A classmate you falsely accused of cheating?
- A parent you neglected?
- A spouse whom you divorced?

Remember the church conflict I described several pages back? It was a wounding experience for me and my family. For the first time in my ministry, I wrestled with the forgiveness factor. Why did I find it so difficult to develop a posture of forgiveness toward those who had hurt the church through the politics of rancor and divisiveness? The process of healing took many months, but I knew that the only way forward was through obedience to Christ.

I could not enjoy His rest if I refused to offer His forgiveness to others. Our family decided that we would live in a posture of forgiveness. We vowed to keep our hearts soft and our arms open.

Now glancing in the rearview mirror, after many years I view the controversy from a clearer perspective. I see how God used the pain, sorrow, and confusion. I had to relearn that my worth was not linked to a church. God released me from a high-profile ministry and enabled me to discern the clear difference between success and significance. I have several friends who are megachurch leaders. They endeavor to walk in the steps of Jesus. Hopefully, they know that success and status can be intoxicating. Whenever we use the yardstick of numeric success as the definitive measure of ministry, then faithful Noah seems like a failure and rebellious Jonah looks like an ecclesiastic superstar preaching to 120,000 people. My identity in Christ teaches me that significance with Him is the most effective detox against the subtle vanity of human approval and achievement.

Consequently, had not the Lord moved me from a church I had served for fourteen years, I would have never experienced the indescribable joy of planting a new church. Furthermore, I would have missed watching Him accomplish more than I could ever imagine among broken and bruised people who are not ashamed of the gospel.

Two years after launching the new church, my treasured mentor and longtime friend, Calvin Miller, asked me to M.C. his retirement luncheon at Beeson Divinity School. Several professors and church leaders testified about the godly impact Calvin had made through his life and ministry as an author, pastor, and professor. I always stood in awe of Calvin's creativity. I often teased him by saying that he wrote books faster than I could read, like the best-selling *Singer Trilogy* and the highly acclaimed *Conversations with Jesus, The Unfinished Soul, When the Aardvark*

Parked on the Ark, and *Life is Mostly Edges*. He was a gifted artist with words. Moreover, he was a beloved friend. In many ways he was the wise pastor that our family often turned to for counsel.

After the luncheon, Calvin expressed his sincere gratitude. We talked privately for nearly an hour until he made a statement that remains fixed in my soul.[24] He said, "I guess you wondered if God was 'picking on you' when you walked through the fire of church controversy." I took a deep breath and admitted that the thought did cross my mind. Calvin smiled and added, "I think it's more likely that God 'picked you'. He picked you for a purpose to testify of His grace through the fire." I hope Calvin was right. I long to personify holy grit. I live and minister in perpetual astonishment of God's grace. More than ever, I understand a paradoxical statement voiced by Charles H. Spurgeon, the peerless British preacher. He said, "The worst days I have ever had have turned out to be my best days, and when God has seemed most cruel to me, He has been most kind."[25]

I imagine that Joseph would agree. God transformed his worst days into his best days because he practiced holy grit and found a way to forgive.

And you? The most grueling task in front of you might not be physical or mental. It might be the spiritual task of exercising holy grit to deal with forgiveness. The issue might be tougher than "can you" find a way to forgive. The real question is, "will you?"

Gritty Take Aways

- **Finding a way to forgive requires the practice of holy grit.** Forgiveness is not for the faint of heart. It involves a costly and courageous choice to release an offense. If we are followers of Christ, we can offer forgiveness because we have been so lavishly forgiven by His death on the cross.

- **Overcoming the hurts that overwhelm you involves erasing false ideas about forgiveness.** Forgiving those who have injured us does not mean condoning their actions or attitudes. It does not pretend that the offense didn't matter. Forgiving does not mean that you will forget the harm. Instead, it means that you choose to offer grace so that the remembering is void of retaliation on your behalf.

- **Viewing your wounds through the prism of God's sovereignty clarifies your perspective.** Joseph could testify that God used for good the abuse and betrayal that others intended for harm. When you see every hardship filtered through God's sovereignty, you see His sovereignty transforming every hardship. Everything that happens to you is not good, but God can bring something good from everything that happens to you. Moreover, His goodness can inspire forgiveness so that you can eliminate grudges against your offenders.

CHAPTER 3

*Nothing is more disastrous than
to study faith, analyze faith, make
noble resolves of faith, but never
actually make the leap of faith.*

Vance Havner

*For everyone who has been born of God
overcomes the world. And this is the victory
that has overcome the world – our faith.*

I John 5:4 ESV

*A faith that paddles about the edge
of the water is a poor faith at best.
It is little better than a dry-land faith
and it is not good for much.*

Charles Spurgeon

Caleb: Sustaining a Resilient Faith

Some days, "holding on" is all you can do. Henry Dempsey understood that maxim better than most. He was the pilot of an Eastern Express commuter plane flying along the edge of the Atlantic Ocean from Portland, Maine, to Boston when he was sucked out of the rear door during sudden turbulence.

The co-pilot radioed the nearest airport for permission to make an emergency landing and requested that the Coast Guard be dispatched to search for the pilot. The co-pilot landed the plane 10 minutes after the incident. To his joy and amazement, he discovered that Henry Dempsey had held on to the outside cable ladder as the plane flew 200 mph. Dempsey had barely kept his head from banging the runway at landing.

Airport emergency personnel rushed to Dempsey's side, ready to whisk him to a nearby medical center. They found, however, that Dempsey's grip on the ladder cable was so tight that it took several minutes to pry his fingers loose.[1] He took "holding on" seriously.

Holy grit involves "holding on" through the perilous journey of life to fortify a resilient faith. Caleb personified "holding on" many centuries before Henry Dempsey. He held on to God's truth when the overwhelming power of perpetual monotony threatened to suck every ounce of hope from his heart. How did Caleb sustain a resilient faith when those around him quaked with fear and shuffled in a wilderness for forty years?

Have you ever wondered why the writer of the Book of Hebrews bypassed Caleb as a person of dynamic faith? Although the faith list in Hebrews is certainly more

Holy grit involves holding on through the perilous journey of life to fortify a resilient faith.

illustrative than it is exhaustive, Caleb appears to sustain a more robust faith than either Barak or Samson.

Caleb was born into a slave family and grew up in Goshen, where hundreds of thousands of slaves lived. He learned the toil of hard labor as a youth and witnessed the bloody penalties administered by Egyptian masters wielding a club and a whip. By the time he was forty, he had dreamed about liberty quite often. On nights when sleep eluded him and babies in nearby tents wailed from starvation, funeral teams transported dead, disease-ridden slaves away for burial. He craved the sweet air of freedom. He recalled stories about a land where his ancestors Abraham, Isaac, and Jacob once lived. A land where a meandering river stretched from north to south and connected two giant lakes. A place dazzling with abundant grain and fruits that teemed with wild game. He imagined how he would feel raising a family and teaching his children their Jewish roots without reprisal from Pharaoh's enforcement squad. He contemplated the ecstasy of living without the dreaded thought of his children being sold and taken away.

When Caleb learned that God ordained Moses to lead the Israelites out of Egypt, he eagerly joined the liberation movement. On his final night as a slave, Caleb obeyed God's instruction to sacrifice a year-old unblemished lamb. He carefully applied its blood to the doorway of his home and faithfully waited for the signal to depart. Soon, he and his family followed Moses and enjoyed the first taste of freedom.Caleb marveled at God's goodness to lead and feed the people. He stood enraptured by God's grandeur as the waters of the sea moved aside, allowing the people to cross over on dry land, making the Egyptian army a rear-view memory.

When the time arrived for Moses to appoint twelve leaders to scout the land of promise, he tapped Caleb from the tribe of

Judah. Caleb was ready. He had set his heart on the land for a long time.Moses assigned Caleb to a reconnaissance team responsible for exploring the terrain of the territory and assessing the size, strength, and location of towns and cities while employing concealment tactics to avoid being captured.

Little did Caleb realize that his faith-filled scouting expedition would lead to four decades of monotony that tested his desire to sustain a resilient faith. How did he endure it? How did he hold on through heartbreaking disappointment? How did he prevail through prolonged frustration in a situation caused by other people's doubt? What kind of grit is necessary to sustain such a dynamic faith?

Unflinching Belief in God's Ability

One of the Bible verses I memorized as a college student is an affirmation that God can accomplish immeasurably more than we can imagine according to His power at work in us.[2]

Two features of this affirmation continue to fuel my life. First, God's ability is never second best. His ability never succumbs to a hopeless situation. He is all-powerful and His strength is imcomparable. Second, God prefers to unleash His ability through the faith of ordinary and imperfect individuals. He delights in displaying His power through those who are eager to trust Him.

After my mother died, my brother and I fulfilled her wish by selling the only house we ever knew while growing up. Letting go of our home place was tinged with sorrow. On the final day, I needed some private time. I walked into the small

God prefers to unleash His ability through the faith of ordinary and imperfect individuals. He delights to display His power through those who are eager to trust Him.

backyard and chased dozens of memories. I imagined all the football games my brother and our friends played. I stared at the drooping powerline that stretched from a transformer to the house. I remembered how often we made sparks fly when the football hit the powerline, making it swing violently. I was struck by the reality that we had no clue about the raw power above us. We were unaware of the unseen energy we played beneath. I stared at the powerline and reflected on years gone by. I wondered how easily I had made the mistake of occasionally worshipping, serving, praying, and leading while blissfully dismissing the astounding power of God. Like too many followers of Christ, I have often played games beneath God's supremacy without praising Him for immeasurable blessings flowing from His boundless power.

One of the many reasons I am drawn to Caleb is because he demonstrates an unflinching belief in God's superiority. He impresses me as a man who believed that God could accomplish insurmountable odds, at improbable times, through unlikely people.

Caleb spent forty days fulfilling his spy assignment. He carefully scouted the landscape, calculating the size of the towns and cities. He assessed the strengths and weaknesses of the inhabitants. He evaluated the fertility of the soil for planting crops and raising livestock. It is reasonable to conclude that Caleb eagerly endorsed cutting and removing the giant cluster of grapes from the Valley of Eschol. Perhaps he and Joshua were the duo who carried the cluster back to Moses.

I once thought that at the end of his mission, Caleb returned to Moses with rowdy enthusiasm and sky-high excitement. Now, I hold a different opinion. I think Caleb was well aware that the majority of the reconnaissance team didn't share the same conviction that he and Joshua held. In all likelihood, the twelve spies discussed their findings and debated the details of the land and its people before they presented their report to Moses. Nevertheless, Caleb's faith in God's supremacy stood firm despite the negative and spineless perspective of the others. His confidence in God's promise was not a brief flame of enthusiasm. It was a steady white-hot furnace of devotion.

All twelve spies testified that the land was abundantly fruitful and "it flowed with milk and honey." The phrase "milk and honey" underscored the promise God made when He commissioned Moses. It symbolized the productivity and richness of the land.[3] All the spies agreed that the land represented what God had promised. Sadly, that was the only positive affirmation voiced by ten of them. Their report dripped with gloom. It was called a bad report because it defamed the character of God.[4] Furthermore, it soaked the people with a fear of failure. Mental health experts assign the term "atychiphobia" to a fear of failure. The term is derived from two Greek words: "atyches," meaning "unfortunate," and "phobia," meaning "destructive" and "irrational" fear.

Having previously witnessed the incomparable power of God, how could the majority of spies dismiss His ability? The answer is not complicated. They allowed the sincerity of their feelings to choke the audacity of their faith.

> *The majority believed there was an obstacle that could not be overcome. Caleb believed there was a God who could not fail.*

They ascribed greater authority to their fear of failure than to their faith in God. A mood of hopelessness prevailed.

Caleb calmed the people and asserted that a victory was certain. His firm reliance upon God contrasted sharply with the majority report. Caleb saw the same challenges as the other ten spies. He analyzed the same landscape. He, too, noticed the giants that occupied the hill country around Hebron. The core difference between the two reports was that the majority believed there was an obstacle that could not be overcome. Caleb believed there was a God who could not fail.

Ten spies, with utmost sincerity, testified that invading the land of promise would be a total failure. They sincerely concluded that victory was unattainable.

Sincerity can be a noble virtue in many situations. A wise physician can use sincerity to ease a tough diagnosis for a patient. A sincere preacher can stir the hearts of seekers with the message of the gospel. Sincerity alone, however, does not guarantee that something is true and right. A person can be emphatically sincere but tragically wrong. We thrive and survive on H_2O, the molecular structure of water. If we sincerely believe, however, that we can drink one hundred percent H_2O_2, we would suffer severe consequences. The difference that one additional molecule makes cannot be changed by our sincerity. After all, H_2O_2 is the molecular structure of hydrogen peroxide.

In the wilderness of Kadesh, the people made a sincere but serious mistake. They exchanged God's truth for sincere fear, and they abandoned holy grit. Their sincerity spawned an open and total revolt against God and a

Sincerity alone does not guarantee that something is true and right.

mutiny against Moses's leadership. A fog of desolation engulfed the Israelites.

James S. Stewart was Chaplain to the Queen in Scotland and professor of New Testament at the University of Edinburg when he delivered the Lyman Beecher Lectures at Yale University. He told a story about Friedrich Moritz Retzsch's painting titled "Checkmate." Retzsch's artistic idea was derived from Goethe's literary character Faust, who made a deal with Satan. Consequently, Retzsch's portrait featured a chess game between

Satan and a distraught young Dr. Faust. The match appeared hopeless for the doctor as Satan leered across the chessboard in anticipation of securing the man's soul. One day a chess master saw the portrait in an art gallery. He intently studied the chess pieces. He calculated moves and countermoves. Other visitors came and went, but he continued to analyze the situation. Long he pondered. Suddenly, with joyful conviction, he shouted, "It's a lie! The King and the Knight have another move."[5]

When all seems futile and hopeless, Satan goads us to think that there is no way out of despair. He mocks us with a scheme of spiritual checkmate. But someone with a resilient faith like Caleb reminds us that the King of Eternity always has another move for those who trust Him.

Wholehearted Loyalty

I traveled to China a few years ago to teach God's Word and encourage nearly 75 Chinese pastors. All of them had enrolled in a biblical exposition class and hoped to evade the suspicious eye of government authorities. Many of them boarded an early morning train at 4:00 to attend the 8:00 class. I marveled at the way the pastors excitedly greeted one another every morning as if they had not seen each other the morning before. I rejoiced because of their deep desire to honor Jesus in attitude as well as action. I also felt convicted while listening to their experience of persecution. The pastors were not ashamed to talk about it. They expected to be persecuted. They were followers of Jesus in a culture that rejected and repressed their faith. Interestingly, I never heard one of them request prayer to be spared from persecution. I did, however, hear them request prayer to remain completely loyal to Jesus during ordeals of persecution. Stunning! How amazing that they treasured loyalty more than deliverance. Their longing was not for status and security. They didn't yearn for health and wealth. Their simple passion and prayer was to be wholeheartedly loyal to Jesus.

I grieved as I considered that in my country, loyalty to Jesus is a waning virtue. Of course, we embrace loyalty to lesser objects of our affection. We display loyalty regarding the banks we use, the retail stores we choose, the restaurants we prefer, and the ball teams we like.

Loyalty itself is not rare in our culture. Loyalty to the Lord, however, is a vanishing discipline. If Caleb were living today, he would be lampooned with satire from some journalists and scalded with parody from entertainers. He would likely be shamed into oblivion on social media. On the other hand, he might have preferred such ridicule compared to the anger he received from his own people. They were enraged by his loyalty to God. They wanted to stone him for recommending that God could be trusted and victory could be achieved.

Caleb can never be accused of lukewarm loyalty. He didn't have a tepid cell in his body. Six times the words "fully" or "wholly" describe how he followed the Lord.[6] There was nothing half-hearted about his faith. Fence-straddling was not a sport he practiced. God's favor rested upon Caleb, and it resounded in the statement, "My servant Caleb has a different spirit".[7] Old Testament scholar Dennis Cole points out that previously only Moses had received the prestigious title "my servant."[8]

God took pleasure in declaring that Caleb exhibited a "different spirit." The Hebrew expression "ruah'aheret" refers to another kind of spiritual attitude and disposition. Caleb was different from the majority of spies because he resolutely and unhesitatingly obeyed God's will.[9]

Echoing Caleb's loyalty is a compelling and costly message for us. A resilient faith that fully follows the Lord extracts a cost in two ways. First, it costs the surrender of our reputation to the renown of God. When we stand before God someday, He will not need to hear about our wounded ego or how a critic hurt our feelings when we spoke up for Him. He won't need to hear how we intended to exemplify holy grit, but circumstances prevented us. Our Father will desire to hear us declare that despite the brutal grind and gut-wrenching battles of life, we put aside the God-denying renown of self for the self-denying renown of God.

Second, it costs us to display risks of faith that others deem unwise and unnecessary. When Caleb pleaded with the Israelites to trust God, they rejected him and tried to kill him. They considered his recommendation perilously foolish and worthy of death. Nevertheless, he knew that the pleasure of God was incomparably greater than the esteem of others.

Wholehearted loyalty is a howling rebuke to spiritual neutrality. It chastens and stings our clever dodging of allegiance to God's truth. Jim Elliot's words have often pricked my apathy. "We are spiritual pacifists, non-militants, conscientious objectors in this battle-to-the-death with principalities and powers in high places…The world cannot hate us, we are too much like its own."[10]

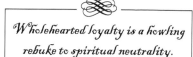

Wholehearted loyalty is a howling rebuke to spiritual neutrality.

Embracing neutrality about clear imperatives of Scripture is like trying to stand in the middle of a highway while faith and culture zoom past us, heading in different directions. We catch just enough blast of faith to appease our culture and just enough draft of culture to minimize our faith.

When the casino gambling industry started to gain a foothold along the Mississippi Gulf Coast, a group of concerned citizens asked me to be their voice of reason against the hype of organized greed. My role, so I thought, was a simple one. First, to present evidence backed by crime statistics that clearly correlated crime and gambling. Second, to make the case about the detrimental economic and moral impact of gambling on all families, especially low-income families. My simple role, however, soon morphed into a giant responsibility.

As weeks passed, I became a target for lobbyists, politicians, and news reporters. I testified before a state legislature committee and much later spoke on behalf of Focus on the Family at the National Gambling Impact Study Commission authorized by then-President Bill Clinton.

I sensed that a showdown was lurking between casino activists and gambling opponents. To mitigate the tension, I decided to host a lunch with representatives from both sides of the aisle. Community leaders, business people, and mayors of cities along the coast gathered in a large assembly room at our church. Toward the end of the meeting, after several leaders on opposite sides of the gambling issue had spoken, one of the mayors walked to the podium and addressed the crowd. "I know the merits and demerits of gambling," he muttered gruffly. "I'm neutral on this issue and I take a middle-of-the-road position." He smiled smugly and added, "I don't give an account to anyone here," as he returned to his seat. The lunch hour was up, and I needed to release those on a tight lunch break so they could return to their jobs. I also felt a reply to the mayor was necessary. So I said, "Thank you, Mr. Mayor. You have my respect, but you also have my dissent. I don't know where you grew up, but where I grew up, the main thing in the middle of the road was a yellow stripe. This gambling proposal does not afford any of us the cowardice of neutrality."

So much for easing the tension! Have you ever voiced a conviction and wondered if you did more harm than good? I wasn't trying to embarrass the mayor. I simply wanted to clear the air of nonsense. Minutes after our meeting ended, a gambling activist greeted me and said, "Pastor, I disagree with your position, but I applaud your response to the mayor. This issue is too crucial for neutrality. You gotta be on one side or the other."

If we serve the Lord wholeheartedly, we might be scared to death half the time and ecstatic with joy the other half, but we won't live with any regrets about our faith.

Enduring a Wilderness

I can't fathom the turmoil that Caleb must have felt. Think about it with me. He acted faithfully. He followed God wholeheartedly. He passionately urged others to obey God. He begged them to seize the appointed opportunity. Still, they refused. Their previous sincerity mutated into scorn. Sincerity coupled with scorn banishes faith. It turns our hearts into a welcome center for spiritual impotence. When scorn toward God's authority is disguised as prudence, it is actually contempt masquerading as wisdom.

Choices carry consequences, and sinful decisions can invite God's punishment. No one twenty years and older would ever enter the Promised Land. They would die in the wilderness. Many of Caleb's friends and acquaintances would be counted among them.

When scorn toward God's authority is disguised as prudence, it is actually contempt masquerading as wisdom.

Year after year, he would hear the news of death. Did Caleb ever hear his friends admit that their decision was wrong? Did he ever lament to God about enduring a wilderness with them? Did he ever cry out to God, asking why he had to suffer for their sinful choice? Did he ever say, "I don't get it, God, I obeyed you. I did what you wanted?"

So what do you do when your emotions are raw with pain? You do what Caleb did. He persevered. He pressed on. He continued to trust God. The seed of holy grit is often nurtured in the crusty sod of a wilderness where robust faith helps it sprout.

Have you noticed that God uses the soil of drudgery and obscurity to strengthen our faith roots? I grew up in South Georgia. I'm familiar with the sandy soil that produces soybeans, cotton, peanuts, and watermelons. Recently, I learned that North Georgia has a flourishing wine industry. If you live in Napa Valley, California, you might wonder how grapes can grow in the red clay mountain area of Georgia. Quaint places like Dahlonega, Ellijay, and Tiger Mountain are now competing against the vineyards of Italy, France, and California. Viticulturists who are involved with winemakers claim that wine is an expression of the soil where grapes are grown. The clay soil is compact enough to allow water runoff so that the roots don't get "wet feet" and dense enough to force the roots to reach deeper and absorb more vital nutrients. This results in healthy grapes that produce unique flavors for muscular and bold wines.

Do you see where I'm going with this analogy? Tough soil can sustain strong roots that yield sweet fruit. Our best spiritual development can occur in a bleak environment. God strengthens our faith

The seed of holy grit is often nurtured in the crusty sod of a wilderness where robust faith helps it sprout.

roots in the soil of wilderness situations to force us into a deeper dependence upon Him. If you are like me, you have to admit that many of your spiritual growth moments have occurred in a wilderness despite your preference for a tranquil garden.

We may wince at the comparison, but we can identify with a bald eagle named Bomber. He was first discovered in Alaska but spent the majority of his twenty-two years in the comfort of a Maryland wildlife center. Bomber was chosen to open the 1984

Olympic Games held in Los Angeles. The plan included circling the interior of Memorial Coliseum to the applause of nearly 100,000 spectators plus millions watching on TV, and then returning to his designated perch. After weeks of aggressive training and dieting, Bomber was prepared for his role. Sadly, Bomber died several days before the opening day ceremony due to a cardiovascular collapse. The years of domestication in a cozy and comfortable environment took a toll on him.[11] We too quickly forget that docile discipleship can't prepare us to be eagles of faith. Couch potato laziness never equips Olympians of God's Kingdom. If we are going to soar as His representatives, we will need endurance training.

> *Couch potato laziness never equips Olympians of God's Kingdom*

Caleb began a journey into the "land between."[12] A transitional place where life is no longer what it had been and not yet what it would become. Behind him rested the memory of scouting the promised land. Ahead of him lay the joyful expectation of living there. Between the memory of his past and the expectation of his future stood a transition called a wilderness. Caleb knew it by the Hebrew word "midbar." It was a desolate wasteland hiding rodents, scorpions, and vipers. A sunbaked place of craggy hills, sandy plateaus, dried creek beds, and jagged mountains. A place where foxes, jackals, lynxes, goats, and ibex competed for food and vultures circled the sky. It was also a place where a soul could easily waste away. Hope could dry up. Perseverance could seem pointless. Monotony could siphon joy and replace it with tedium.

I've never been to the wilderness of Sinai. I'm not sure I want to go. I have been through a few spiritual wildernesses, and I'm sure I don't want to go back. What about you? If you've experienced a spiritual wilderness transition, you probably don't need me to describe it. If you haven't, I'm not sure that I can sufficiently emphasize how it gnaws at your soul. How it consumes your emotions. How it sifts and grinds your fortitude, testing the mettle of your faith. My wilderness duration was minuscule compared to Caleb's forty-year ordeal, so I wonder what kind of skill set is needed to sustain a resilient faith for decades.

I imagine one of the first things Caleb needed was a daily refill of holy grit. He knew that faithful intimacy with God refreshed his passion to persevere. Aren't you glad that God offers free refills of His grace and strength? Fullness from Him equips us to overcome pitfalls and challenges. After all, the wilderness can dehydrate dreams and wilt determination.

No one conquers a spiritual wilderness without consistent refills from the Redeemer.

It can play tricks on our memory and delude our devotion. Caleb took big gulps from the well of God's promise because God alone can slake our thirst in a wasteland. No one conquers a spiritual wilderness without consistent refills from the Redeemer, who enables our will to persevere.

Caleb also needed a heavy-duty focus to counter all the distractions surrounding him. The Israelites moved aimlessly. They flittered indecisively. They vacillated between worshipping God and bowing to Baal, battling enemy nations and fighting among themselves. Maintaining a godly focus required Caleb to exercise an indisputable resolve.

Soon after President Lincoln appointed Ulysses S. Grant as commander of all Union armies in the Civil War, Grant launched a major attack on Gen. Robert E. Lee's Confederate Army of Northern Virginia. Lee surprised Grant, however, by luring him into battle in a wilderness area nine miles west of Chancellorsville, Virginia.[13] The first two days of the Wilderness Battle proved to be a bloodbath. Bullets whizzed back and forth like sheets of pelting rain. Thousands of Union soldiers died and thousands more moaned in the dense thicket where they fell. Despite heavy casualties, General Grant told a young reporter for the *New York Tribune* to let President Lincoln know about his resolve. When the reporter arrived at the White House, he requested a private meeting with the President. With deep pathos, the reporter said, "General Grant told me to tell you that whatever happens, there is to be no turning back."[14] Similarly, Caleb held a focus that would not allow retreat or defeat. Although his peers wanted to turn back, his focus never allowed such absurdity.

There was one more thing Caleb needed in the wilderness. He needed to set a worthy example. He couldn't change the faithless decision of his peers or the sentence of death God levied upon his generation. He could, however, set a righteous standard for future generations.

Will read Caleb's story again and again and admired his faith. Just as Caleb set a compelling example, Will set a valiant example. No one in his small town expected him to amount to anything but ordinary. During the day, he made and repaired shoes. By night he learned Latin, Greek, and Hebrew. He obeyed God's call and believed that everyone in every nation should have an opportunity to respond to God's grace.

When he spoke at a minister's meeting, his message met severe criticism. However, historians later referred to it as "the first and still greatest missionary treatise in the English language."[14] Will moved to India and spent forty years facing hardships and helping people know Jesus. During the first year, he grieved the death of his five-year-old son and the escalation of his wife's mental illness. As years passed, he endured financial crises and threats from Hindu extremists. He worked tirelessly to abolish infanticide and the bondage of women. He founded Serampore University, one of the first degree-awarding institutions in India. In addition, he translated and supervised the translation of the Bible into forty distinct dialects and languages.[15] Will was known formally as William Carey. His legacy continues to inspire resilience in hundreds of thousands who follow Christ. He said if anyone wished to write about his life correctly, they should indicate how he could "plod" and "persevere" in his labor for the Lord.[16] Caleb likewise chose to plod and persevere despite living with a generation beaten by pessimism and sin. He led by godly example, sowing seeds of faith and hope that would not reach maturity until years later.

Leadership expert John Maxwell cited a survey indicating how people become leaders. He revealed that five percent become leaders by natural gifting. Ten percent become leaders because of a crisis. Significantly, eighty-five percent become leaders due to the influence of another leader. Maxwell emphasized that "it takes a leader to raise a leader."[17] Lots of young eyes were fixed upon Caleb as a leader worth emulating. His life was a testimony of a passionate will to persevere. He never compromised a standard of holy grit.

Rewards of Faith

An epic moment seldom gives advanced notice, but once it occurs, everything changes. The unforgettable moment when the Israelites crossed the Jordan River to enter the Promised Land signaled a turning point and a new era. Just as the Israelites transitioned from decades of slavery to freedom by leaving Goshen, they transitioned from years of wandering to a season of establishment by crossing the Jordan.

After several notable battles in the new land, the moment arrived when Caleb requested from Joshua the inheritance God had promised him.[18] This is one of my all-time favorite passages in the Old Testament because it testifies to the holy grit that sustained Caleb's faith. The reward of a resilient faith is greater than we imagine for several reasons.

First, the reward is exponentially richer than the accumulated years of hardship. Caleb was eighty-five. We don't expect octogenarians to attempt rigorous exploits, much less engage in combat with well-trained enemies. No doubt, the wilderness climate had bleached his beard and eyebrows white. His face was stained a leathery bronze. His muscular biceps looked like weary balloons lined with slightly bulging veins. His knees sounded like the crackle of dried leaves. Inside his aged frame, however, beat the heart of a gritty warrior who would not relinquish his dream or mothball his faith until he stood upon the land God promised him.

As I write this chapter, I'm in the last year of my sixth decade. I've watched too many men and women put their faith on a shelf as they grow older. They velvet wrap their faith and treat it like a museum piece worthy of admiration but useless for application. They complain about the inability to do what they once could do with ease as if physical dexterity determined the ultimate purpose of life and faith.

I'm unsure of Kelly's age when we first developed a friendship. He looked eighty, but he might have been younger. His body was severely deformed and contorted by long years of cervical dystonia, rheumatoid arthritis, and spinal kyphosis. He was confined to a bed that he could not leave without the help of nurses. Nevertheless, every day he would ask his sister to place the phone beside his ear and make calls so he could encourage people. He called me every month, and the joy in his voice was captivating. One day as I sat beside his bed, I leaned in. I asked if he ever felt angry about his condition. He replied, "Of course, I've had moments of frustration. I used to dream of marriage and having children. But somewhere, years ago, I decided I had a choice. I could fume with resentment or I could pray with faith. So every day, I have God's blessing of confinement. I've been granted the privilege of lying in bed so that I can pray for you and tons of other people." Suddenly, I felt small, like a toddler in the presence of a spiritual giant. Kelly's testimony has long challenged me to remember that the reward of faith immeasurably transcends the harsh circumstances of our years.

When John Steinbeck embarked on a journey across America, he weighed the risk of traveling alone thousands of miles. He admitted that

> God's blessings always flow to those who risk all that they are for all that He is.

the security of home and family were tempting substitutes for uncertainty and danger. But he lamented the sterile domestication that replaces a life of precarious adventure. Steinbeck noted that with the passing years, so many men "begin to pack their lives in cotton wool, smother their impulses, hood their passions, and gradually retire from manhood."[20]

None of that tame behavior would have appealed to Caleb. His retirement plan was saturated with risk. He must have known that God's blessings always flow to those who risk all they are for all that He is. Caleb claimed that at eighty-five, he was as strong as he was at forty, "for war and for going and coming."[19] He was not boasting about his ability. He was emphasizing that the same God who "kept him alive" was the One who could empower him to conquer the hill country.

This points to a second reason the reward of faith is greater than we can imagine. It can make the giants we face look like an incidental obstacle. Caleb didn't forget about the Anakim. He had known they lived in the hill country of Hebron for more than forty years. He didn't fear them either. He asked Joshua to grant the land around Hebron as his inheritance from God so that he could drive out the giants. How refreshing that an old veteran like Caleb personified resilient faith full of holy grit! Hebron was not a golf course of lush fairways. It was a steady climb to an elevation of 3,000 feet on igneous rock. Upon completion of his ascent, Caleb faced three notorious giants named Sheshai, Ahiman, and Talmai. They were powerful warriors and sons of Anak.

Undaunted by the obstacles, Caleb defeated the giants and established Hebron as his home base. It wasn't by accident that Caleb selected Hebron. Hundreds of years earlier, Abraham erected the first altar of worship for God at Hebron. Caleb may have taken deep satisfaction in his victory, knowing that the site of the first worship in the Promised Land was once again a sanctuary for God.

When the road behind has left you weary, and the trail ahead seems too far, ask your Father for resilient faith. He will not fail you!

If the Lord allows me to reach the age of eighty-five, I want to have a resilient faith like Caleb. I want my passion for God to be greater than any time before. I don't want to look in a mirror and hear the man staring back at me ask, "What happened to you? Why did you settle for a lukewarm devotion? Why didn't you trust God with more abandon?" Well-intentioned friends have occasionally suggested that I should "eat, drink and be merry" and turn down the grit dial. They advise me to play it safe more and to risk less. They mean well, but I can't locate in Scripture a "release from duty" clause due to age or hardship. I realize the day may come when I have to gum my food, wear incontinence briefs, and use tennis balls at the base of my walker. So what? I still want to have a heart that beats strong for Jesus and a gritty faith that runs straight towards the giants.

I think you understand what I'm saying. You've felt the same tension between risking yourself for Jesus and protecting yourself from harm. Let me be clear. I'm not advocating recklessness. I'm calling for bold grit. The kind John Bunyan demonstrated when he wrote, "I am for going on and venturing my eternal state with Christ. Whether I have comfort here or not. If God doth not come in, thought I, I will leap off the ladder blindfold into eternity, sink or swim, come heaven, come hell. Lord Jesus, if thou will catch me, do! If not, I will venture for thy name."[20]

I am convinced that Bunyan shared the same holy grit that sustained a resilient faith like Caleb's. Will you venture all for Jesus too? Can you hear His gracious whisper to persevere with holy grit? When the road behind has left you weary, and the trail ahead seems too far, ask your Father for resilient faith. He will not fail you!

Gritty Take Aways

- **A resilient faith requires holy grit to pursue God's truth through long and grueling years.** Although God's ability never succumbs to anything you perceive as an impossibility, your distrust and doubt carry dire consequences. Sincere people can deny His ability and resist His purpose. Sincerity can never be the defining standard of right or wrong.

- **A resilient faith is decisive. It repudiates fence-straddling and vacillation.** It embraces wholehearted loyalty. It is a rebuke to spiritual neutrality. When we serve God wholeheartedly, we can be scared to death half the time and ecstatic with joy the other half, but we won't live with regrets about our faith.

- **Enduring a protracted wilderness necessitates regular refills of holy grit.** God's refills equip you to overcome challenges and pitfalls. They also sharpen your focus and enable you to set a compelling example of devotion.

- **The reward of a resilient faith lies in the determination not to abandon God's promise despite our circumstances.** Enduring a protracted wilderness requires a passionate will to persevere. The reward rests in the satisfaction that you faced the giants with holy grit and finished strong in the journey of life.

CHAPTER 4

*I can plod. I can persevere in any definite
pursuit. To this I owe everything.*

William Carey

*And let us not grow weary of doing
good, for in due season we will
reap if we do not give up.*

Galatians 6:9 ESV

*Thus working and waiting belong together.
In combination, they will deliver us both
from the presumption which thinks we can
do everything and from the pessimism
which thinks we can do nothing.*

John R. W. Stoll

Elijah: Overcoming the Urge to Quit

Tenacity circulated through his veins. Relentlessly, day by day, year after year, he persevered. He accomplished a feat that experts considered unattainable. Forty-five thousand people roared their applause. The President and Vice President stood and cheered with profound admiration. Fans at Baltimore's Camden Yard interrupted the baseball game between the Orioles and the Los Angeles Angels for twenty-two minutes of wild ovation. Players on the opposing team lined up to shake his hand. Dozens of sports journalists described with glowing appreciation an epic September evening when Cal Ripken Jr. broke Lou Gehrig's baseball record for consecutive games played.

I watched the game on TV and marveled at Ripken's astounding grit. How could he play so passionately for so long at such an exhausting competitive level?

When the thunderous acclaim diminished, Ripken and his Oriole teammates finished the game against the Angels. Ripken, however, was not finished with his streak. He continued to play, never missing a game until he reached 2,632 consecutive games. Four United States Presidential elections and sixteen years passed between the beginning and the end of Ripken's historic feat.

So I wonder. Why did the man show up to play and never miss a game despite ankle, hand, and wrist sprains during the streak? What drove him to endure the pain and keep going when he suffered a broken nose? How did he overcome the urge to quit when he herniated a disc and hyperextended an elbow?[1]

Quitting is a common experience. It can be appropriate for the right reason. Quitting harmful habits, violence, abuse, and hateful rhetoric is noble and desirable. Quitting on God is not.

So when we read about a mighty prophet named Elijah, sulking in a cave and ready to throw in the towel on God, what's going on? If a mighty prophet struggled to conquer an urge to quit, how do ordinary believers like me and you fight the "give-up" syndrome?

Prophets of God were peculiar men, and Elijah embodied a peculiarity like few others. He strides through the pages of the Old Testament like a titan of holy grit. Nothing he did was conventional. Situations and circumstances that would make other men turn back made Elijah run forward. He erupted in public places like a

If a mighty prophet struggled to conquer an urge to quit, how do ordinary believers like me and you fight the 'give-up' syndrome?

surprising thunderstorm on a summer afternoon. He voiced God's truth with the impact of a lightning bolt. Elijah was a rugged outlier who learned to trust God in the backwoods of Gilead. He preferred solitude but obeyed God's call to be a point man. He refused to dance to the tune of political propriety, choosing instead to march in cadence to God's command.

Elijah lived during the reign of King Ahab, one of the most infamous and powerful rulers in the history of Israel. In the category of wickedness, Ahab topped the list. Ahab's wife, Jezebel, was the daughter of a Sidonian king.[2] She was a devout worshiper of Baal, the deity of rain and fertility. Along with her husband, she promoted the idolatry of Baal throughout the Northern Kingdom. Jezebel terrorized God's prophets, and many of them hid in fear. She tolerated no rivals to her idol.

Into that dark, oppressive time, Elijah burst on the scene. He confronted Ahab with a bold announcement that neither rain nor dew would touch the land until he commanded it.[3] Elijah wasn't bragging. He wasn't posing. He stated a promise based upon the authority of the one true God. But hold on! Did Elijah miss the breaking news report about Ahab and Jezebel? Did he realize the power they wielded? Did he understand that they took delight in exterminating opponents? Would it have made a difference if he did? I doubt it. Elijah doesn't strike me as a man who easily trembles under pressure. The years he spent trusting God in the shadow of obscurity prepared him to confront a king openly, face to face.

Treasures From a Creek Bank and a Widow's Cabin

Shortly after Elijah stunned Ahab with a holy declaration, he departed back into obscurity. God directed him first to Cherith and then to Zarephath. Cherith was a small meandering creek that cut a deep ravine into the crusty landscape. Elijah remained concealed at Cherith, relying upon God to feed his soul and nourish his body. God provided water from the creek, and He directed ravens to bring him food.

If you like extreme austerity, then dining with ravens is for you. I confess that my faith would need a nuclear dose of grit if God asked me to eat road kill from scavengers. Rotting armadillo meat would trigger my gag reflex. Crushed rabbit carcass would be a severe challenge to my taste buds. If I had somehow managed to swallow it, I think it would come back up quickly.

That's why I am captivated by Elijah's ready acceptance of God's provision. He obeyed God without reservation. I can think of several horrible diets, but putrid "hors d'oeuvres" from a raven's beak would top my list of nauseating cuisine. Elijah didn't try to bargain with God. He didn't propose an "if-then" deal. You know how that works. I do too. It's one of those begging pleas like, "God, if you will provide exactly what I desire, then I'll go where you direct and do what you say." Elijah didn't seek an easy way to obey. He sought to obey without the easy. His commitment presents a profound example of deep devotion united with steadfast dependence. Devotion and dependence are inseparably linked. We are never intimately devoted to God unless we practice steady dependence upon Him.

Soon the drought that Elijah predicted took a toll. The earth baked and the vegetation withered. Cherith creek dried up. Elijah endured the nasty food, but he couldn't survive without water. Cherith served as a spiritual boot camp that prepared him for the next assignment.

Obedience at one level opened an opportunity for obedience at another level. God commanded Elijah to move to Zarephath, a town on the coast of the Mediterranean a few miles south of Sidon. It was a hostile territory ruled by Jezebel's father. A place where Baal worship dominated. The Hebrew word "Zarephath" refers to the process of melting, refining, and testing.[4] God sent Elijah to a refining place to test his character and melt away the impurities of self-sufficiency.

Pause for a minute and slip your feet into Elijah's sandals. Consider that God has directed you to a place known for rampant evil. You could face execution if someone informs Jezebel about your location.

Furthermore, God tells you that a defenseless and vulnerable widow will help you. Oh, there is one more consideration. You have been ordered to stay there indefinitely. How would you handle the challenge?

A conscientious man like Elijah would be reluctant to impose upon a poor widow. He may have wondered why God called him to burden someone so destitute. Nevertheless, he trusted the competency of God even if he couldn't comprehend the plan of God. Elijah located the widow near the town gate of Zarephath and asked for water and bread. It was a modest request, but her resources were meager. She possessed only a paltry portion of flour and oil to cook bread that she and her son could eat. Starvation loomed heavy. She fully expected to die. Elijah exhorted her to use what she had, and God would supply what she lacked. Was he irrational? Her situation was practically hopeless. She faced her last meal. It is a testimony to Elijah's grit that he pressed the widow to use all she had. It is a testimony to the widow's faith that she complied.

The person who trusts God completely is always refined by God exquisitely. God heats the furnace of holiness to remove contaminants that mar His design. He monitors the temperature. He never raises it above a limit and never drops it below a necessity until He sees a reflection of His character.

> *The person who trusts God completely is always refined by God exquisitely.*

Through the refining process, the widow discovered that the handful she offered became a perpetual mouthful. Likewise, Elijah discovered that the Mighty God who directed ravens to bring food at Cherith could also sustain him through a penniless widow at Zarephath.

The drought continued as the months accumulated. The first year morphed into a second year. Elijah knew that survival wouldn't be easy, but he couldn't anticipate the widow's heartbreak over the sudden death of her son. She made a common accusation and drew an erroneous conclusion about the tragedy. She accused Elijah of being a harbinger of judgment. Then she concluded that the death of her son was directly connected to the sins of her past.

Elijah wisely responded. He didn't rebuke her. He didn't give five reasons why her anger was inappropriate. He didn't try to correct her faulty theology of suffering. Elijah embraced the woman's grief to the point of bypassing Hebrew custom. Levitical tradition prohibited a man of God from touching a corpse, but Elijah decided that a child's life mattered far more than a religious custom. He took the boy in his arms and carried him to a room for prayer. Holy grit involves not only the ability to carry the anguish of a tragedy but the compulsion to ask God to use it for His renown.

Consequently, prayer was the first recourse for Elijah. Sadly, for many of us, prayer is a last resort. If other options fail, then we pray. We treat prayer as a final possibility instead of a first necessity. Elijah stretched himself over the boy three times. The physical repetition may have emphasized persistence, but Elijah's prayer was not based upon the efficacy of human contact. It was based on the reality of God's power. Consequently, Elijah's plea to God was intensely personal. He cried, "O Lord, **my** God."[5] A deep relationship with God can never be a secondhand affiliation marked by cold and pedantic prayer. It's essential to keep in mind that God's response to our requests is always predicated upon four words: "according to His will."[6] Elijah boldly prayed for God to breathe life back into the child. And God dramatically did it. The privilege of "asking" God for a miracle carries the corresponding responsibility to leave the "answering" with Him.

Steven Curtis Chapman and his wife, Mary Beth, have modeled faith, hope, and love for thousands of people around the globe. Steven's award-winning songs have poured truth into my heart for many years. But Mary Beth's story about the tragic death of their daughter Maria reached a deeper place inside me. When Maria lay lifeless in the trauma room of the medical center, disconnected from the life support equipment, Steven cried emphatically, "Oh God, breathe life into Maria! You can bring her back to life! Please bring her back to life."[7]

Mary Beth knew that God could work a miracle. She also knew that God had answered in a way they didn't want. She softly whispered to Steven as he stood weeping over their daughter, "We've got to let her go, Sweetie. It's time to let her go." To this day, their story wrecks me. It challenges me to understand that when we choose to see God's fingerprints upon our most unasked-for moments, we can endure our hardest sorrows.

God owns the editing rights to all our prayers. He adds, deletes, and rearranges as He desires. God allows us to steward the stories that don't end the way we desire. He invites us to see that the blessing of prayer is far more than receiving the answers we want. It is being the kind of person God can trust with the answers He gives.

> *When we choose to see God's fingerprints upon our most unasked-for moments we can endure our hardest sorrows.*

A Fight for Truth

A few miles from my home stands a historical marker commemorating the site of America's longest bare-knuckle boxing match. In July, 1889, beneath a scorching Mississippi sky, John L. Sullivan fought Jake Kilrain in an epic heavyweight showdown. Kilrain drew first blood in the sixth round with a roundhouse punch to Sullivan's head. Unfazed, Sullivan countered with a flurry of powerful jabs. By the thirtieth round, Sullivan's punches had taken a toll on Kilrain. Blistered from the summer sun, the boxers continued blow by blow until the end of the seventy-fifth round. That's right! Seventy-five grueling rounds. A doctor informed Kilrain's managers that their man could die unless the slugfest stopped. Kilrain conceded defeat, and Sullivan was hailed as the victor. Ironically, both boxers were arrested a few of days later and fined for illegal bare-knuckle fighting.

As significant as that contest remains for boxing enthusiasts, it pales in comparison to the showdown centuries earlier between Elijah and Ahab at the base of Mt. Carmel. At stake was not a struggle between two bare-knuckle opponents, but a showdown between a godly prophet and an idolatrous king. It was a fight between truth and deception.

Whether we like it or not, there is a cosmic fight we cannot avoid. There is an ongoing battle between good and evil. A ruthless war between the kingdom of God and the kingdom of Satan. C. S. Lewis saw this clearly when he wrote, "There is no neutral ground in the universe; every square inch, every split second is claimed by God and counter-claimed by Satan."[8]

The religious climate today might be as competitive and bizarre as it was during Elijah's time. We live in a culture that resists an exclusive faith in the one true God of Scripture. Our culture prefers a belief that all religions lead to God. Prevailing public opinion regards the exclusivity of faith in Christ as intolerant. Similarly, the conflict between Elijah and Ahab involved a battle between competing beliefs.

During the year when God ended the drought, He commanded Elijah to contact Ahab again. Tension bristled between the prophet and the king. Elijah proposed a face-off at Mt. Carmel and requested Ahab to bring his 450 prophets of Baal and 400 prophets of Asherah, the female cohort of Baal. Ahab must have been delighted to invite all Israelites to the event. He expected a decisive victory with 850 to 1 odds in his favor.

An enormous crowd gathered as Elijah shouted a penetrating question: "How long will you go limping between two different opinions? If the Lord is God, follow him; but if Baal, then follow him?"[9]

If you've ever wondered why the worship of Baal was so attractive to the Israelites, there

> *Whether we like it or not, there is a cosmic fight we cannot avoid. It is an ongoing battle between good and evil. A ruthless war between the kingdom of God and the kingdom of Satan.*

are two key reasons. First, there was a compelling magnetism toward idolatry. Its captivating lure was an appeal to satisfy their sinful and selfish nature. Second, they believed the lie that Baal worship would satisfy their quest for sexual fertility and provide them economic prosperity. From our perspective, it seems illogical that they would dismiss the blessings of the Sovereign God who delivered them from slavery, made them fruitful to multiply, and established them as a nation. Indeed, idolatry is illogical, but the idols of money, sex, and power are no less alluring to us than they were to the ancient Israelites.

The Israelites limped or "wavered" between God and Baal because they believed one religion to be equally as true as the other. Elijah challenged them to make a decision. His "either-or" test remains applicable today. Either the truth claim of God's revealed Word is accurate, or the truth claim of any other religion is accurate. Both can't be accurate because God's truth contradicts the other.

Let me hammer a point. We dare not limp between truth and falsehood. We must not vacillate between holiness and iniquity. Any attempt to merge walking with Christ with kneeling for Baal is illegitimate. A decisive break must occur. A verdict must be reached. A choice must be made. Sadly, if we choose a lifestyle of idolatry, it will leave us spiritually lame and eternally alienated.

Elijah dared the people to face the truth by challenging Baal to consume a sacrifice with fire. The prophets of Baal placed oxen for sacrifice on the altar. They began to pray. From morning until noon, they pleaded and circled the altar. Elijah provoked them by suggesting that Baal might be meditating or perhaps taking a bladder break. Infuriated by the taunt, the prophets howled and gashed themselves. By midafternoon, hundreds of bloodied and exhausted devotees limped around a sacrifice void of fire. Baal was proven to be a mute idol.

It was Elijah's turn. First, he rebuilt the altar of the Lord using twelve stones representing the twelve tribes of Isreal. The broken altar symbolized Israel's departure from God. Next, he dug a trench around the altar and told the people to fill it with water three times. The wood and oxen were soaked to rule out any accusation of trickery. Notice the contrasts: saturated wood and oxen on God's altar versus the dry wood and oxen on Baal's. A trench flooded with water compared to Baal's arid trench. Elijah, a solitary prophet of God, calmly standing against 450 sweaty, edgy, and mortified fanatics of an idol.

Elijah prayed for God to be glorified by igniting the sacrifice. His pressing desire was for the Israelites to encounter the one true God.[10] Suddenly, the fire fell. It incinerated the sacrifice, the altar, and the water in the trench. God invaded the moment. The guilty Israelites fell on their faces confessing Him as Sovereign Lord. God proved to be the righteous stalker who answers prayer, performs miracles and pursues rebels who are reluctant to worship Him. The stunned prophets of Baal were slain.

If you're wondering where grit comes into this picture, consider two things: First, it took an arsenal of grit for Elijah to maintain courage against Ahab and Jezebel. Second, Elijah demonstrated godly perseverance after the conflict by praying and seeking rain seven times. He didn't give up when his servant reported six times that "there was nothing" on the horizon that remotely looked like rain.[11] Storm clouds soon gathered, however, and the refreshing rain fell just as God promised. But dark clouds of dismay accumulated in Elijah's soul.

A Warrior's Resignation

Elijah barely found time to celebrate the victory before Jezebel unleashed her rage. She dispatched a message notifying Elijah that he would be executed within twenty-four hours. His courage evaporated. His faith wilted. Elijah panicked and ran for his life. He fled 115 miles from Jezreel to Beersheba in southern Judah. Then he continued his fugitive flight at least 250 miles further south to Mt. Horeb.

It's not easy for me to examine the defects, faults, and flaws of my heroes. I prefer to focus on their gritty exploits rather than their spineless foibles. I shudder with grief when I picture the Reformation giant John Calvin endorsing the execution of Michael Servetus. I wish Calvin would have championed religious liberty. I stand with Calvin in his defense of biblical truth against Servetus' heresy, but not at the expense of Servetus' life.[12] I didn't like discovering the emotional pain and financial suffering A.W.Tozer caused his wife.[13] I wish he would have communicated affection to her and provided for her in an exemplary manner. I hold a longstanding admiration for British missionary C. T. Studd and his heroic effort to spread the Gospel in China, India, and Africa. Early in my ministry, I read about Studd's gritty faith, and it stirred a fire inside of me. Especially when he wrote, "Some wish to live within the sound of church or chapel bell, but I want to run a rescue shop within a yard of Hell."[14] I was saddened to learn that he depended upon morphine during the last few years of his work.[15] I wish he could have carried out his missionary duties without drug addiction.

Yes, it's difficult for me to admit that all my heroes have flaws. I understand that they all have feet of clay. I prefer to imagine Elijah standing against Jezebel's indictment as a braveheart for truth. I don't want to think of him groveling in fear and running for cover. I favor Elijah the stalwart instead of Elijah the quitter.

I am encouraged to read, however, that Elijah had a "nature like ours."[16] I'm profoundly grateful that the New Testament provides that insight. Otherwise, we might elevate Elijah beyond measure. We might forget that he was subject to the same limitations and temptations that we face. He knew the exhilaration of trusting God, but he became familiar with the desert of despair.

Can't we confess that we have walked in Elijah's tracks of brokenness? Have we not allowed our holy grit to dissolve also? We have all, at some moment, lost our resolve to persevere, and we have submitted our resignation. If not out loud, at least under our breath, we have whispered, "God, I'm burned out. I quit. I'm done. No more."

Elijah's life is like an advanced placement class in radical grit. Few believers today could pass the exam at Cherith creek, much less the exam at Mt. Carmel. Elijah's strength makes me step back in awe, but it's his weakness that invites me to draw close and listen to the whisper of God.

Elijah's crisis of faith can teach us vital lessons about our struggles and the factors that tempt us to give up and quit on God.

Fear: Elijah was understandably afraid. Who would fault him for avoiding an execution date with Jezebel? Fear clouded his focus. He was so blinded by her threat that he couldn't perceive God's guidance. Fear has a way of taking our faith captive and making us detainees in a cell of intimidation. Fear forces us to repeat Elijah's three-word resignation: "It is enough."

I admire people who are characterized as fearless. I cling to the truth that "perfect love cast out fear."[17] I don't know about you, but I'm a work in progress regarding that truth. Fear still sneaks up on me. Total eradication of it has not occurred in my life. I am discovering, however, that I can fear less even when I'm not completely fearless.

Fear is deceptive. It will lie to us. Fear can persuade us to doubt the goodness of God and give up on life. Fear was choking a lady who called me

> *Fear is deceptive. It will lie to us. Fear can persuade us to doubt the goodness of God and to give up on life.*

in the middle of the night. I groaned a groggy "hello." I'm not lucid when I'm awakened from a deep sleep. She apologized and said she didn't want to reveal her name. Then she unloaded a bombshell question, "If a Christian commits suicide can they go to Heaven? I need an answer because I'm holding a loaded .38 caliber pistol, and I'm ready to end my life." I gathered my thoughts and quickly prayed for wisdom. She continued, "I love Jesus, but I'm tired of living with fear and discouragement." "Okay, I hear you," I replied. "Let's just tap the brakes and exhale. May I ask you something? If you love Jesus and you trust His purpose for you in Heaven, what keeps you from trusting His plan for you here on earth?" She didn't reply. She continued to elaborate on the fear and condemnation that tortured her. I listened and when I thought it was appropriate, I tenderly asked again: "If Jesus can take care of your future, why can't you believe He can take care of you here and now?" "I . . . I . . .I don't know," she sobbed. Seizing the moment, I emphasized her significance and worth. I explained that Jesus was able to sustain her on her worst days and longest nights. He wanted her to choose life even when it was hard and dark. She apologized again for calling. I prayed with her but worried about what she might do.

Several Sundays later, a guest introduced herself at church. She shared her name and smiled. "I'm the person who called you in the middle of the night. I was at the bottom," she said. "I was hopeless and thinking dark thoughts. When you reminded me that Jesus was enough, I realized how much I wanted to live for Him. He is greater than my moods and bigger than my fears." I hope she learned that she was not alone in her struggle. Some of God's most faithful servants have plunged into the depths of spiritual anguish. Similarly, Elijah was in a dark place spiritually. His fear was bigger than his faith.

Fatigue: "Fatigue makes cowards of us all," wrote Gen.

George S. Patton in a 1944 memo to inspire the U. S. Third Army during World War Two.[18] Several years later, legendary NFL Coach Vince Lombardi drilled that statement into his Green Bay Packers. Whether it involves a military operation, a professional football objective, or any significant decision, fatigue can shape the outcome. Fatigue can turn effectiveness into hopelessness. It can enslave the brave and annihilate the great.

Fatigue pushed Elijah to give up and resign. Think with me. He carried the post-traumatic stress of a death threat. He suffered the prolonged physical exertion of running, walking, and climbing 115 miles over rocky and challenging terrain. Weary and exhausted, he crawled under the canopy of a juniper tree. He told God to take his life and allow him to die. Elijah was a burned-out and broken man.

Nobody is immune to the peril of fatigue. Fatigue forces us to make mistakes of judgment. When nothing is left in our tank, we give in to bad decisions. Fatigue causes us to draw faulty conclusions. Elijah's devotion to God's call faded. His passion for God's glory dissolved. Fatigue can be a debilitating dictator. If we let it dictate what we know about God, then what we know about God will become hazy and obscure. Fatigue crumbled a hard-core spiritual warrior like Elijah and turned him into a jaded prophet who would rather give up than go on.

Erroneous Comparisons: The marriage of fear and fatigue gives birth to erroneous comparisons. We begin to evaluate our devotion to God based on the devotion others have for God. Erroneous comparisons only lead to disappointment, and disappointment can lead to detachment from God.[19] Elijah declared, "I am no better than my fathers."[20] What did he mean? Was he expressing

The marriage of fear and fatigue gives birth to erroneous comparisons.

humility? Was this a confession of his mortality or was there something else in his statement? Perhaps it was an admission that compared to Abraham, Isaac, and Jacob, he was not their equal. However, God never required him to be a better leader than his forefathers. I have a hunch that Elijah was so deep in despair that he no longer saw himself as a champion of the faith. He conceded that his accomplishments were no better than his forefathers. He had hoped the victory over the Baal prophets and the shocking display of God's power would win the day for righteousness and spark a spiritual awakening throughout the nation. But nothing changed. Wickedness still ruled the land with Ahab and Jezebel continuing their reign of corruption. Elijah thought he was the only prophet left who fought for the truth.[21] He couldn't shake the reality that his zeal for God failed to ignite a movement of holiness. Elijah erroneously gauged his service and devotion to God as a futile effort.

The problem with comparing ourselves to others who serve and minister is that we use inaccurate scales that yield incorrect conclusions. The scales of human opinion can neither measure devotion to God nor assess the eternal impact of such devotion. Sadly, Elijah weighed his worth based on how his ministry impacted the nation, and he drew the wrong conclusion. He believed that his service to God had minimal value and marginal impact. He saw himself as no better than all the others who had tried and failed. He surrendered the flag of determination and raised the flag of resignation.

God's Plan for Recovery

Elijah could not heal himself. The worm of despair had chewed a hole into the core of his soul. The damage ran too deep for band-aid solutions. The rugged outlier who seemed invincible was curled up and waiting to die. The prophet who once personified grit was ready to quit. He needed an intervention from God. He required a recovery.

If you have ever trudged through a winter of despair, you wonder if the healing springtime will emerge. The icy winds of gloom darken the days and lengthen the nights. You doubt that a seed of hope could sprout through the frozen barrenness of a heart that once throbbed with unfettered faith.

I hold an affinity for spiritual strugglers who rest beneath shrub trees of honesty. Let me explain. I'm not referring to whiney babies who are quick to complain about the rigor of godliness. I'm not talking about sideliners who evaluate discipleship as if it were a religious game. I'm alluding to what Theodore Roosevelt called "the man who is actually in the arena." Specifically, "the man whose face is marred by dust, and sweat, and blood who . . . if he fails, at least fails while daring greatly, so that his place shall never be with those cold and timid souls who know neither victory nor defeat."[22] Elijah knew both victory and defeat. Victory at Mt. Carmel and defeat in the wilderness of Sinai. One of the main reasons I appreciate spiritual strugglers is that at least they are in the fight. They are not spectators in the grandstand. They face daily battles against guilt and shame. They wrestle against the strange bedfellows of self-sufficiency and self-condemnation. They know the temptation to quit and the urge to succumb to the emptiness.

God will not mock your feelings. He will repair your damaged emotions. He will not malign your scars. He will point you to the scars of His Son.

Elijah qualified as a spiritual struggler during his life. He needed an injection of holy grit. He was wounded and confused, but God met him at the point of his pain and sorrow.

Perhaps you identify as a spiritual struggler right now. You feel like your best days are behind you. You think your future is dim and trending toward darkness. You admit that you've enjoyed spiritual victories when you knew God was pleased. But now, the dogs of despair are attacking. You wonder if you matter. You doubt that the battle you wage against sin is worth the agony.

Please lean in and let me encourage you to look beyond your fears, fatigue, and frustration. Focus your attention upon the God who passionately pursues you. He adores you. He refuses to abandon you. God will not mock your feelings. He will repair your damaged emotions. He will not malign your scars. He will point you to the scars of His Son. I have sat where you sit. I am all too familiar with the dungeon of depression. Like you, I have spent my share of days beneath the cover of bewilderment. But I am delighted to tell you that God prepares a sanctuary of recovery for you just as He did for Elijah. The God who applied His remedy to Elijah's misery offers the same healing steps for us today.

Rest: God created rest. He ordained it as necessary for our recovery. God allowed Elijah to sleep. Sleep plays a key role in physical health, mental acumen, and emotional wellness. Sleep helps our body repair and it improves productivity in our mind. It also releases serotonin hormones that can affect our mood and restrict depression.

Elijah did not know about the medical benefits of sleep or rest. That's ok. He benefited from it anyway under God's watch care. Elijah didn't need to challenge one more prophet of Baal. He needed to rest. He didn't need to perform like a crusader. He needed to relax like a child. Performance-based spirituality is not the same as faith-based spirituality. Performance-based spirituality relies upon the good works you do. Faith-based spirituality relies upon the good work God does through you. Performance-based spirituality views God's grace as an award to be earned. Faith-based spirituality realizes that God's grace is a gift to be received. Performance-based spirituality leads to exhaustion. Faith-based spirituality leads to renewal and refreshment.

Jesus invites all of us who are worn out from the treadmill of religious activity to come to Him. He promises rest not only for today but forever. He bids us take His yoke and learn His ways so that we can experience true rest. And one more thing: His yoke is easy on our shoulders and His burden is light.[23] His yoke is never a slavish burden for performing. It's a harness of grace for living.

> *Performance-based spirituality leads to exhaustion. Faith-based spirituality leads to renewal and refreshment.*

Nourishment: The critical role of nourishment in recovery is well documented from Harvard Medical School to Baylor College of Medicine. Research indicates that the relationship between the gut and the brain confirms that healthy nutrition decreases the risk of depression and enhances positive mental health.

Stop once again and look at Elijah under the juniper tree. Yes, he needs rest, but he also needs nourishment. God knew exactly what Elijah needed. That's why He directed an angel to compel the prophet to "rise and eat." Some friends in my academic circle doubt the intervention of an angel. They contend that it was another traveler who exercised kindness and left Elijah a bread cake and water. Certainly, God could have inspired someone to do that, but I believe He sent an angel just as the text states. If God could direct the birds to take food to Elijah, couldn't He also direct an angel to minister to him? So let's not miss the obvious point that God intimately provided nourishment for Elijah's recovery. It is somewhat startling, however, that when Elijah finished his food and drink, he went back to sleep. He was so spiritually numb and emotionally traumatized that an angelic encounter didn't move him. Can't we see ourselves in Elijah's predicament? Can't we notice a yellow caution light flashing a message? If we are not careful, despair can raise a hardened wall between us and God. It can make us indifferent to His presence, insensitive to His truth, and unaware of His grace. Nevertheless, God did not respond with condemnation. His love was not altered by Elijah's lethargy. His grace was not restricted by Elijah's disregard.

Dialogue: Elijah traveled forty days and nights until he reached Mt. Horeb. He must have meandered because if he had walked fifteen miles each day, he would have covered the two hundred and fifty miles between Beersheba and Mt. Horeb in approximately sixteen days. The symbolic aspect of "forty" may have been Elijah's attempt to replicate the forty years the Israelites spent in the wilderness and to imitate Moses' forty days on Mt. Horeb when God renewed His covenant.

The first thing Elijah did when he arrived at the mountain was to locate a cave. He was still a broken man in need of recovery. He wasn't crawling into a cave simply to file a "hurt feelings' complaint." He was deeply dismayed by despair and searching for a refuge. If Elijah longed to die in a cave, his wish was challenged by a voice from God. It was a six-word question, "What are you doing here, Elijah?"[24] God established a dialogue with His disillusioned prophet. Whether it's in a dreary cave on a mountain or in a messy closet at home, God can speak to our hearts and begin a dialogue for recovery.

God nudged Elijah toward self-examination. He forced Elijah to answer why he had camped at Mt. Horeb. During a crisis of faith, we must analyze our despair and face the truth about ourselves. Elijah needed to ask himself the hard question about what he was actually doing at Mt. Horeb when, in fact, the work of obeying God was back in Israel. Furthermore, God's question compelled Elijah to search his heart and answer why he was hiding. Was he hiding because of Jezebel's threat? Did he have any idea that God was arranging a defining moment of intervention that would restore his fellowship?

Elijah's reply to God overflowed with raw emotion. Phil Ryken, president of Wheaton College, analyzed Elijah's condition and noted that "spiritual depression is hard to shake. It's not a twenty-four-hour virus." [25] Elijah expressed his pent-up feelings to God. His dismay that Israel had abandoned God's covenant laws, his loneliness in the battle for truth, and his perception that he was indispensable, poured out of his soul. Despair gluts itself on inaccuracy and exaggeration, and Elijah's reply contained a bit of both.

God listened to Elijah. He listens today when the turmoil inside of us boils over. He listens when we inaccurately complain about life's trouble. He listens when we exaggerate our own importance to His mission and

Whether it's a dreary cave on a mountain or a messy closet at home, God can speak to our hearts and begin a dialogue for recovery.

when we think that we might be indispensable to His work. God is the perfect counselor. He listens wisely. He discerns our thoughts and speaks to our hearts.

God instructed Elijah to stand before Him on the mountain. The weary prophet lingered in the shadow of the cave. He was reluctant to obey. Suddenly, a violent wind roared across the craggy crest of Horeb. Stones tumbled like an avalanche down the mountain. The ground began to shake from an earthquake and boulders cascaded from their lofty sockets. Lightning flashed and fire pierced the eerie darkness. But the Lord was not in the wind, the earthquake, or the fire.

Elijah might have misunderstood a few things about God.

He may have thought that God's sensational display of power was the way He always worked. Elijah had witnessed stunning miracles. He saw God raise a dead child back to life. He watched God incinerate a water-soaked altar of sacrifice in the blink of an eye. God is able to do exceedingly more than we can imagine. He can create something out of nothing and create nothing like it. He can place a sphere in the void of nothingness, populate it with life, and allow that sphere to move in an orbit at 67,000 mph while spinning at nearly 1,000 mph. He can turn a sea into a highway. He can clothe dry bones with flesh. He can make the dead breathe life again. God can work just as powerfully, however, in quiet, simple, and subtle ways that Elijah had overlooked. God spoke to the heart of His weary and wounded prophet in the "sound of a low whisper."

The King James Version translates this phrase as "a still small voice." It is often difficult to render the Hebrew text exactly into English, but a literal translation would be "a voice, a gentle one, a whisper."[26] It was God's holy hush that wooed Elijah out of the cave to experience a breakthrough from despair. The tender voice of God speaking to his conscience enabled him to fight the urge to quit.[27] Our Heavenly Father still works His miracles in the mundane of life. Rather than through a roaring wind, He whispers life-changing truth through His infallible Word. Instead of an earthquake, He moves through the tremors of our perseverance. In place of fire, He purifies our grit through the inferno of His holiness.

A Hero's Reassignment

The difference between resigning and "re-signing" is drastic. Elijah arrived at Mt. Horeb resigning, but God arranged a "re-signing" event for him. God knew exactly what Elijah needed to get off the bench of despair and back into the game of life. God never runs out of a mission for us to tackle. He always reserves a place on His team for broken believers. His recovery plan is usually a protracted process rather than a quick fix. God seldom rushes us through therapy.

Following the surgical repair of a rotator cuff and a labrum tear in my shoulder, I endured three months of therapy at a rehab clinic. I was

God always reserves a place on His team for broken believers.

sure that Attila the Hun was my therapist. Progress was slow and painful. One day Attila was stretching my shoulder, and I was having profane thoughts about revenge. He must have read my facial expression. He calmly said, "I know you don't like this. I know it feels like torture. But unless I stretch your shoulder properly, you will never use it effectively. You will never regain full range of motion." I reluctantly complied, allowing Attila to continue as I pondered the phrase "full range of motion."

Similarly, God stretches our faith so that we might regain the full motion of our devotion. It hurts as He pushes and presses us to reach farther in obedience and go deeper in devotion. Elijah had allowed his memories of yesterday to grow bigger than his vision of tomorrow. He thought his best days were done. God promised, however, that better days were ahead. Does this sound familiar in your journey? Does it touch a sensitive nerve in your soul? Do you stare at your past more than you dream about your future? Admittedly, we all find it hard to embrace change as we consider what God might require of us. But our next steps are never more full of hesitation than they are full of God's presence. If you have waded through the swamp of despair and are ready for a reassignment, God will faithfully remind you that:

- Your greatest journey can be taken.
- Your best story can be written.
- Your bravest battle can be fought.
- Your strongest witness can be voiced.
- Your proudest moment for God's glory can be realized.

I suspect that Elijah was surprised to hear God say, "Go anoint Hazael, Jehu, and Elisha."[28] The time for healing had arrived. A new ministry day had dawned. Cave days were over. God expected Elijah to get back in the game and exercise holy grit. God expects the same from me and you when we languish on the sidelines. Elijah needed to return to active duty. God granted him a new assignment. In leaving Mt. Horeb, he was not putting a period on the last sentence of his ministry. He was beginning a new chapter of holy grit.

God gave Elijah three tasks that profoundly impacted the Israelites. First, Elijah found Elisha and anointed him as his successor. Elisha's personality was different, but his prophetic influence was similar to Elijah's. Second, Elijah, in partnership with Elisha, commissioned Hazael as King of Syria. Hazael would become an instrument of judgment that God used to punish Israel. Third, Elijah, indirectly through Elisha, appointed Jehu as an instrument of judgment upon the throne of Ahab and Jezebel. The arrogant king and idolatrous Queen would meet a violent death after a life of corruption and murder.

Furthermore, God encouraged Elijah to realize that he was not a lone warrior for righteousness. God had 7,000 other bravehearts that were faithful in the fight and had not surrendered to Baal.

Few of us will become national leaders like Elijah, contending for truth against the politics of power and the policies of perversion. Few of us will champion the trustworthiness of God against idolatrous vendors of depravity as heroically as Elijah. Ninety-nine percent of us, however, will battle dismay and despair like Elijah and feel the urge to quit. Don't yield to that temptation. Resist it. Fight it with holy grit and persevere. "Be steadfast, immovable, always abounding in the work of the Lord, knowing that in the Lord your labor is not in vain."[29]

Gritty Take Aways

- **God monitors the heat in the furnace of your refining.** He never raises the temperature above the limit we can bear, and He never lowers it below a necessity that shapes our character. Consequently, prayer should be our first priority rather than our final possibility.

- **Fear and Fatigue can hijack your faith and make you a detainee in a cell of intimidation.** Fear will lie to us and persuade us to doubt the goodness of God. Fatigue forces us to make mistakes of judgment, and it obscures the truth we know about God. The union of fear and fatigue gives birth to erroneous comparisons that tempt us to quit trusting God.

- **Performance-based spirituality will exhaust you, but faith-based spirituality refreshes you.** God listens to our frustrations and our brokenness without berating us. Rather than endorse our resigning, He empowers us for a "re-signing" event. God stretches us during our cave days to enable us to regain the full motion of our devotion to His will. He bids us report for active duty and to resist the urge to quit.

CHAPTER 5

Deity nursing from a young maiden's breast. Could anything be more puzzling- or more profound?

Ken Gire

And Mary said to the Angel, "How will this be since I am a virgin?" And the Angel answered, "For nothing will be impossible with God."

Luke 1:34, 37 ESV

Mary should be honored, but the Father, the Son, and the Holy Spirit should be worshiped.

Brant Pitre

Mary: Moving Beyond Impossible

I love Christmas, but it departs too quickly. I relish the nativity decorations, the trees blinking with red, green, and amber lights; the old carols and new songs; church preschoolers loudly singing "Joy to the World," and quiet evenings staring into our fireplace while chasing memories. I especially cherish the festive gatherings with our family and friends.

It seems, however, that no sooner have we reached the peak of exhilaration on Christmas Day than we shuffle through the valley of exhaustion on the day after. Then, poof! The Christmas season is gone for eleven more months.

One of the things most difficult to keep is what I call "just rightness." It's that brief sliver of time when everything seems good and right. That full feeling when joy overflows, laughter resounds, bear hugs abound, and love consumes every millimeter of your heart. It's that moment when everyone longs to put time in a bottle and preserve the fleeting ecstasy of that "just rightness."

I have felt it in my soul when I gazed at my wife, my adult children, their spouses, and my grandchildren. I have sensed the Spirit's holy whisper of "just rightness" at Christmas. A reminder that it's all about "Immanuel," God with us. How staggering to consider that God embodied an infant. The Creator of humanity indwelled human flesh in an obscure Jewish town called Bethlehem. The Hebrew word "Bethlehem" means "house of bread." How astonishing that He who is the "Bread of Life" took nourishment from his mother's breast. The infinite Redeemer rested in the arms of a finite virgin.

Theologians refer to the birth of Jesus as the "incarnation" because He became flesh. Although He existed eternally before time, He subjected Himself to time and the limitations of a human body. He was fully human, yet fully divine and completely sinless.

The birth of Jesus struck me in a profoundly practical way one Christmas Eve Sunday. Having celebrated worship with our church family, I loaded my worn-out car to join my wife and children who were waiting for my arrival at my parent's home. Halfway through the long drive, on a monotonous two-lane highway through small towns near the Okefenokee National Swamp, my radio began to fade. Then my car lights grew dim.

The alternator on my clunker was dying, and so was my hope of getting home. I coasted into a dilapidated one-pump gas station and asked an elderly man if I could make a call on his landline phone. He quipped, "Make it quick. I'm closing my shop. It's Christmas Eve, young man. Don't you know?" I called my dad to explain the situation, "Looks like I'm stranded, Dad. The alternator on my car is dead. I can't get home so I'll just . . ." But before I could finish, he replied, "Since you can't get to us, I'll get to you. I'll throw my tools in the van and be there soon." I sat in the car shivering as the night grew cold. Waiting. Praying. The rescue my dad provided seemed to illustrate that first Christmas and the helplessness of humanity.

We could not get to our Heavenly Father, but He could get to us! In a dilapidated Jewish town in a clunker of a stable, "God with us" became a confirmation that God was for us and He would rescue us.

Obviously, Jesus is the *sine qua non* of Christmas. He is the main attraction, without which there is nothing. His mother, Mary, however, deserves prominent recognition for her supporting role.

I confess that there is more to Mary than I can describe. She is genuinely appealing but profoundly perplexing. She is iron tough with grit but velvet-tender with grace. She is both a role model of surrender and a paragon of mystery. She was favored highly in Heaven but regarded lowly in Nazareth. She birthed the baby who would split history into before and after. She gave Him glory to be born, and He gave her the honor to be born again. No other female in art history has been so well documented as Mary.[1.]

I am troubled, however, by ecclesiastical art and sculptures that portray Mary as a joyless and stoic icon daintily posing as an insignificant relic. I

Mary displayed a spiritual passion fueled with holy grit.

agree with Scot McKnight, who described Mary as "wiry, and spirited and resolved and bold and gutsy." [2] I am convinced that Mary, described in the Gospels, was prayerfully surrendered, optimistically obedient, compassionately faithful, and far more dangerous than dainty. She displayed a spiritual passion that was fueled with holy grit during a time when women were seldom esteemed and rarely heroic. What I'm admitting is this: Mary intimidates my devotion, but she inspires my resolve. She demonstrates what it means to move beyond the impossible.

Beyond Impossible Selection

On New Year's Day in 1903, no one could remotely imagine how the year would unfold. In literature, Jack London published his novel, *The Call of the Wild*. In transportation, the Model A car, a two-seater runabout, was manufactured and sold by the Ford Motor Company. In sports, the first World Series of baseball was played between Pittsburg and Boston. In the candy business, Milton Hershey mass-produced his milk chocolate bar.

Few people knew about the two sons of a conservative pastor in the Church of the United Brethren in Christ. The sons, Wilbur and Orville, lived in Dayton, Ohio, and nursed a dream to move beyond the impossible feat of building and producing heavier-than-air flying machines. A widely held scientific opinion boasted that it was practically impossible for man to fly in a machine. *The New York Times* lampooned the idea and stated in an October, 1903 editorial that it might take "the combined and continuous efforts of mathematicians and mechanicians from one million to ten million years to succeed at flying."[3]

Almost nine weeks later, on a cold, blustery December day near the Outer Banks of Kitty Hawk, North Carolina, the Wright brothers made the impossible give way to the possible and became the first men to fly.

Historian David McCullough described it as "one of the turning points in history, the beginning of change for the world far greater than any of those present could have imagined."[4]

Indeed, the Wright brothers' achievement signaled an epic turning point in history, but it bows to the seminal event in the life of a Jewish girl named Mary in a town called Nazareth.

God selected Mary to embrace the impossible. He picked her to conceive a child apart from sexual intercourse with a man. He chose her to nurture the child and to help him to grow and mature into manhood. God designated Mary to be the mother to the Savior of the world.

But why Mary? Why not someone more influential, more popular, and highly educated? Why not someone politically connected who could leverage social status and sway people in positions of power?

Mary wondered the same thoughts. When the angel Gabriel greeted her as the "favored one," she reacted with perplexity and anguish. She never considered that being highly favored by God could invite high anxiety. Gabriel didn't give Mary a quick-step instruction manual about how to respond when you're a "favored one." The favor of God can look different than we imagine. The expression itself is tossed around loosely by speakers and writers. It is often drained of its God-initiated and God-ordained purpose.

The favor of God is inseparable from the grace of God. To be highly favored is to be divinely graced. God's grace cannot be earned, hawked, or bought. It can only be received even if we can't comprehend why He treasures us so much.

Mary was engaged to Joseph. She anticipated her wedding day. She had refrained from sexual activity and remained a virgin. So how could Mary explain that she was pregnant? How could she persuade Joseph

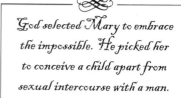

God selected Mary to embrace the impossible. He picked her to conceive a child apart from sexual intercourse with a man.

to believe the impossible? Everyone in the village of Nazareth would mock him and scorn her. Tongues would wag. Gossip would grow. Everyone knew it was impossible to be pregnant without a sexual encounter.

I once talked about Mary with a skeptic. He argued that if Mary had been a true believer, she would not have been fearful of the message and the Angel from God. I understood his point, but I knew that faith wrapped with apprehension is stronger than agnosticism dressed with swagger. One of Mary's most admirable qualities is that, despite her bewilderment, she trusted God's truth anyway. What we do with our "anyway" moments can reveal the measure of our faith. How we respond can be a tipping point leading to either a breakthrough of belief or a breakdown of hope.

Mary was well acquainted with her Jewish heritage. She absorbed the stories of Moses, Joshua, David, and Ruth and their "anyway" moments. Like when Moses stood with a daunting sea before him and Pharaoh's army angrily approaching behind him. Impossibility loomed large, but Moses trusted God "anyway," and the water parted. Like when Joshua faced a walled fortress at Jericho. The mission seemed insurmountable. How could a wall fall by marching around it and shouting? But Joshua obeyed God "anyway" and secured the victory.

Mary must have treasured listening to her father or a rabbi tell how David, on an ordinary day, delivered food to his brothers on a battlefield and maneuvered past sideline warriors quaking in their armor to view a boisterous, spear-wielding giant. And against all odds, how David used one of five smooth stones and relied upon God "anyway" to conquer Goliath.

Surely Mary enjoyed hearing about Ruth's "anyway" moment. How Ruth, while nursing grief and facing famine, believed God could direct her steps "anyway" and how He arranged Boaz of Bethlehem to be her husband.

Mary may have considered herself to be an impossible choice to be the mother of the Son of God, but she punctuated her "anyway" moment with

What we do with our "anyway" moments can reveal the measure of our faith.

an exclamation of obedience. She hurried to visit her relative Elizabeth, who was six months pregnant. When Mary arrived, the sound of her voice prompted the baby inside Elizabeth to leap and bounce. Elizabeth's baby would be John the Baptist, the forerunner of the Messiah. Mary's baby would be Jesus the Messiah, the Anointed Christ.

Mary erupted with a heart-overflowing celebration of worship. Her song of praise has been called "The Magnificat," derived from the Latin word for "magnify" because she exclaimed, "My soul magnifies the Lord."[5] The message is revolutionary. The lyrics throb with subversion. God is the subject of nearly every verb.[6] He lifts the overlooked. He champions the oppressed. He treasures the humble. He shows mercy to those who fear Him. He scatters the proud. He removes rulers from thrones. He dismisses the rich and embraces the poor. He fills the hungry with fullness.

Her song was a serenade to God. It glorified God's justice and extolled His ability to turn the world upside down and to set it right side up. Mary and Elizabeth enjoyed several months of fellowship and prayer with each other until Elizabeth gave birth to John, and Mary returned to Nazareth. She needed to explain her situation to Joseph.

Can you imagine the agonizing conversation irritated by tears and fears? Although the New Testament provides no record of anything Joseph ever said, he doesn't strike me as a man given to outbursts of rage. Not someone who would shout demeaning accusations. He seems more reserved and pensive, like a quiet and kind man that held strong convictions. The single adjective that described Joseph was "righteous."[7] He was someone who would do the right thing for the right reason. F. D. Bruner points out that the biblical application of "righteous" carries a vertical sensitivity to the will of God and a horizontal sensitivity to people.[8] Joseph personified both dimensions.

According to Jewish law, Joseph had two choices. The first and most common choice for men in that quandary was to take the woman before the religious leaders who could either shame her publicly for adultery or give her the death penalty by stoning. The second choice was to privately give the woman a divorce. Joseph's love for Mary permeated the pain he experienced. Rather than allow religious authorities to condemn her or execute her, Joseph decided to treat Mary respectfully and secretly divorce her.

He couldn't bring himself to believe Mary's story about an angel's visit. He couldn't until the evening when an angel of the Lord appeared to him and convinced him to take Mary as his wife. Together, he and Mary said "yes" to God's purpose and "no" to their plans. Holy grit means trusting God when everything in you screams that it's impossible.

Believing God's purpose can require us to relinquish our

expectations of the way things ought to happen. Our presumptive opinion must yield to God's perfect wisdom. We learn to trust God best when we obey him regardless of the complications.

If Mary needed confirmation that she was God's selection to be the mother of the Messiah, He provided it in several ways. Beginning first with Gabriel, God reminded Mary that nothing was impossible for Him. After all, if God could

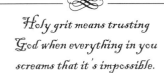

Holy grit means trusting God when everything in you screams that it's impossible.

create everything that exists out of nothing, then the miracle of the virgin birth would pose no difficulty for Him.

Next, God prepared Elizabeth to announce that Mary was the mother of the Lord. Later, He sent an angel to persuade Joseph to take Mary as his wife because she fulfilled the prophecy that a virgin would conceive and bear a son who would save people from their sins.

More confirmation arrived when Mary gave birth in Bethlehem. Shepherds testified to her that an angel declared that they could find the Savior resting in a manger, wrapped in swaddling clothes. God sent common shepherds to gently remind Mary that her baby would be "God with us" to ordinary people.

In addition, God provided confirmation forty days after Jesus' birth when Mary and Joseph went to the Temple for a purification ceremony. A man named Simeon, presumably a priest, but certainly a devout and righteous man, was assured by the Holy Spirit that he would not die until he saw Christ, the Lord's anointed one. When his eyes fell upon Jesus, he announced that he could die in peace because he saw in Jesus the salvation for both Gentiles and Jews. Likewise, a prophetess named Anna declared that Jesus was the redemption of Israel.

Perhaps a year and a half after Jesus' birth, God arranged

one more stunning confirmation. He directed an astronomical anomaly to guide Magi from the East to the home of Mary and Joseph. When the Magi saw the child Jesus, they fell down in worship and offered priceless gifts of adoration.

Mary might have wondered why the Magi would travel so far. Why they would risk the wrath of Herod. Why Gentile men would seek a Jewish Messiah? She could not deny, however, God's corroboration of her role as mother to the Savior of the World.

Maybe you're thinking you don't have Mary's measure of holy grit. You don't believe you could maneuver past the land mines of impossibility. I have the same reservations. The indecision that paralyzes your devotion threatens my passion also. Thankfully, God does not

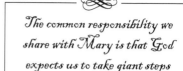

The common responsibility we share with Mary is that God expects us to take giant steps of surrender just like she did.

expect us to be Mary. He has a different role for us to play and a different race for us to run. The common responsibility we share with Mary is that God expects us to take giant steps of surrender just like she did. If God selects you for a hard mission, will you accept it regardless of the complications? If He requires you to relinquish your reputation for something that seems impossible, will you trust the Lord and reply, "may it be done to me according to your Word?"[9]

I believe Mary would affirm a conviction Fleming Rutledge stated in her book *Advent: The Once and Future Coming of Jesus Christ*. She wrote, "It is beyond the capacity of human parents to produce a child who is God. Humankind cannot bring forth a Jesus. Only God can do it. Only God will do it. Only God! Mary was just as helpless as Joseph to make this happen. The human impossibility is overcome by the irresistible power of God."[10]

Beyond Impossible Parenting

My children are adults now. They are parents guiding their children to passionately follow the Lord. My wife and I rejoice to watch the way they intentionally shepherd the heart of each child. The pleasure of parenting can be rewarding beyond expression. It can also be agonizing beyond explanation.

I find rich delight in reviewing "remember when" moments. The unforgettable "weh-weh" through puckered lips at birth. The breathy burst of cooing and giggling. The first wobbly steps with facial expressions of surprise. The world-stopping moment when the words "ma-ma" and "da-da" came forth. The timid delight on that day when we released them to grade school. Birthday parties. Quiet walks in December snow on the hills behind our home. Vacations at the beach. Dogs named Soldier, Pepper, and Deacon. Their duck named Skippy. Daily routines of homework, high school projects, and extracurricular events. Her beauty in a pageant gown. His celebration in a sweaty baseball uniform after a championship game. Prom and graduation. Engagement and wedding. A thousand undeserved blessings as a parent.

But anyone committed to being an edifying parent knows it is a two-sided coin. The flip side of pleasure and reward is exhaustion, distress, and a strange kind of pain that defies definition. Psychologist, James Dobson, hit the bullseye some years ago when he said, "Parenting isn't for cowards."[11]

Effective parenting requires a gutsy and godly resolve. Children don't exit the birth canal with a booklet for easy parenting in their hands. Tough decisions have to be made. A parent must hold difficult conversations about ethical choices, temptation, disappointment, social pressure, groupthink, and dozens of "what if" situations.

Courage is a high-quality virtue optimized by most mothers.

A mother carries a child for several months in her stomach but forever in her heart. My daughter knew of a mother who fought a terminal battle with cancer. The pain was crippling. During the final weeks of her life, when her legs would not allow her to stand, she would crawl into the rooms of her children to pray over them and kiss them good night.

Now that several years have passed, the children are teenagers who cannot forget how their mother crawled to them inch by tortured inch to demonstrate her love. They will never forget the dauntless devotion of their mother's sacrifice.

A virtuous mother is a:

- *Grace Dispenser*
- *Wound Kisser*
- *Hug Lover*
- *Nurse Practitioner*
- *Security Guard*
- *Attitude Adjuster*
- *Kitchen Manager*
- *Fashion Analyst*
- *Speech Teacher*
- *Bible Reader*
- *Story Teller*
- *Prayer Partner*
- *Career Guide*
- *Mercy Maker*

Effective parenting requires a gutsy resolve. Children don't exit the birth canal with a booklet for easy parenting in their hands.

Whenever I hear someone say, "Pastor, don't you think it was much easier being a parent in the first century than today," I wonder what kind of an alternate reality they embrace. The only easy parenting is irresponsible parenting that neglects the physical, spiritual, and emotional health of a child. Dereliction of duty is not hard, but modeling holy grit as a mother is exceedingly difficult.

Mary faced what seemed to be an impossible parenting task. Surely she asked herself, "How do I raise the Son of God?" "How do I guide the steps of a child who will be called the Savior?" Surely Mary begged God to provide wisdom for teaching, courage to fight anxiety, and stamina to endure the rigors of motherhood.

So, let's look at three occasions in the Gospels that provide snapshots of Mary as a parent. The first picture occurred in the Temple when Jesus was 12 years old.[12] Here's the context. Mary and Joseph attended the Passover celebration every year in Jerusalem. Quite often, nine or ten large families would travel together in a caravan. When the week was over, Mary and Joseph headed back to Nazareth. They mistakenly assumed that Jesus was traveling with their caravan and enjoying conversation with his friends. At the end of the day's journey, Mary and Joseph realized Jesus was missing. Any parent who has ever lost a child temporarily can understand the choking anxiety Mary felt. I accidentally left my four-year-old son asleep on a church pew one night. I thought my wife had taken him home after church. She assumed that he was with me. The church security director began turning off the lights and locking the doors as I left. When I arrived home, my wife asked about our son. The expression on her face indicated a serious problem. I jumped into my car and hurried back to the church, where I found him curled up and sleeping soundly in a dark sanctuary. I was overjoyed with relief. Mistakes can happen. There is no need to conclude that Mary and Joseph were careless parents. After asking others in the caravan about Jesus, they returned to Jerusalem searching for him. They found him in the Temple engaged in dialogue with the teachers. Men who had spent years studying the law and prophets of Scripture stood amazed at Jesus' insight.

Can you imagine Mary's sigh of relief mingled with frustration? Can you perceive her composed intensity as she interrupted the discussion and motioned for Jesus to come to her side? Perhaps she gave him an affectionate hug followed by firm hands on his shoulders as she said, "Son, we have been so worried. Why have you treated your father and me this way?" In fairness to Mary's perspective, she felt that Jesus had distressed and embarrassed them by his absence. In fairness to Jesus' perspective, he felt Mary and Joseph should have known that His father's house and His father's mission were an ultimate priority. He explained that his priority was "necessary." The divine necessity that compelled Jesus at twelve years of age continued to compel Him throughout his ministry and ultimately to the cross.

As Jesus and his parents headed back to Nazareth, Mary "treasured up" the moments in her heart. Like an attentive mother, Mary deposited scores of details in her memory. The Greek word for "treasured"

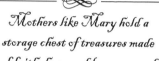

Mothers like Mary hold a storage chest of treasures made of faith, hope and love wrapped with ribbons of holy grit.

refers to guarding and keeping something safe.[13] Mary couldn't know all that lay ahead, but she preserved holy moments so that one day, when she needed to connect all the memories, she would have a portrait that was clear and full of glory forever. Mothers like Mary hold a storage chest of treasures made of faith, hope, and love and wrapped with ribbons of holy grit.

A second snapshot occurred at a wedding celebration in Cana[14], a town in Galilee about nine miles north of Nazareth.[15] Jesus was thirty years old and beginning his ministry.[16] He and a few disciples were guests at the celebration where Mary may have been coordinating the catering and hospitality. During the celebration, the wedding party ran out of wine. Such a predicament threatened disruption of festivities and signaled a social embarrassment that could make the groom's family liable for a lawsuit.[17] In an attempt to avert a crisis, Mary informed Jesus that the family had no more wine. Mary did not ask Jesus to perform a miracle. She only informed him about a problem and hoped He could help.

Jesus' reply sounds abrupt and impolite. He said, "Woman, what does this have to do with me? My hour has not yet come." He was not being harsh. He was emphasizing that Mary's claim on Him was subordinate to the primary claim of obedience to His Father. This was a seminal moment for Mary as a parent. It was a turning point between a devoted mother and a dutiful son. No doubt she was proud of Jesus, but she could not continue to relate to Him like most mothers related to their sons. She could no longer view Him as only her son. He was the Messiah, God incarnate, the Redeemer on a mission to conquer sin and death and rise again triumphantly.

Mary's response testified to her sterling temperament. Rather than take offense at her son's terse statement, she honored Him by telling the servants to "do whatever He tells you."[18] She didn't know what Jesus was going to do, but she trusted Him completely.

Mary realized Jesus could take a bad predicament and make it right and honorable, but she likely didn't know in that instant He could turn water into wine. On the back side of His first miracle, Mary understood that her relationship with Him had changed irrevocably. Jesus' power was a stunning sign persuading Mary and His disciples that the laws of nature yield to His command. Mary may have sighed and smiled as she stood mesmerized while contemplating a deeper meaning of "God with us."

The third glimpse of Mary as a parent revealed her protective motherly instinct in what seemed to be an attempt at intervention. Jesus was ministering in Capernaum, the hometown of Peter and

Andrew, His first two disciples. While He was teaching in a local house, a huge crowd gathered to listen. It grew so large that He had neither the time nor the opportunity to eat. When Jesus' family heard that news, they concluded that it was necessary to intervene and take Him home.[19] This incident stirs more questions than it provides answers. Did Mary initiate the rescue? If so, why? Did Jesus' brothers persuade Mary to join them in an intervention? Did Mary get drawn into the middle of a sibling conflict? Since honor and shame were superlative values in Jewish culture, did Jesus' family attempt to guard their reputation at the expense of His mission?

When His family arrived, they remained outside but sent a message to Him inside. The people in the house passed along the message that His mother and brothers wanted Him to come outside. Jesus explained that His mother, brothers, and sisters were those who embraced God's will.[20] The will of God involved believing Jesus was the Anointed One sent by God. At this point in His ministry, His brothers did not believe He was the Messiah.[21] They knew Him as a carpenter and a stonemason. Cutting wood, crafting yokes, chiseling stone and crafting jars made a lot more sense to them than speaking about a transcendent kingdom. Furthermore, Jesus was the oldest child and served as the head of the family after Joseph died. His place was at home, they likely insisted.

The family tension must have been a troubling burden for Mary. She had to listen to the well-intended skepticism from her children while offering Jesus support regardless of their reaction. Given Mary's personality profile in the Gospels, I wonder if she followed her adult children to the house where Jesus was teaching, to be a peacemaker. I suspect that Mary wanted to de-escalate a potential conflict and calm the friction. Of course, it is also possible that she was so worried about the stress Jesus faced that she joined her children in an attempt to coerce Him to rest His mind and reconsider the pace of His ministry.

Whatever the reason for Mary's involvement, it would be safe to conclude that a godly mother never stops parenting, no matter how old her children become.

Beyond Impossible Heartbreak

The way of holy grit is pockmarked with heartbreak. It extracts a toll to be paid in a currency of sorrow and suffering. The connection between holy grit and heartbreak is unilateral. Heartbreak can happen apart from holy grit, but holy grit always involves heartbreak. As much as we might admire holy grit, it can never be a casual stroll along life's garden trail accentuated by fragrant blossoms and all things pleasant.

Mary must have suspected that she would have to travel that path. She must have reflected upon Simeon's prophecy and often wondered what he meant by "a sword will pierce through your own soul."

Mary had seen the gladius sword strapped to the hip of a Roman soldier. The gladius was a short double-edged sword sharp enough to pierce through the body and heavy enough to crush a skull. She knew it represented pain and death. The rattle of the sword in her soul grew loud on that Sabbath day in Nazareth when Jesus stood in the synagogue to read from the scroll of Isaiah. Mary was likely attending since Jesus was speaking. Her son was a hometown favorite.

At first, everyone applauded Him. They were amazed at His eloquence until He stated that He fulfilled the messianic prophecy. When he emphasized that God's grace could reach the Gentiles like the widow at Zarephath and Naaman the Syrian, it was too much for the synagogue leaders. In a rage of hostility, they drove him out of Nazareth and attempted to kill him.

Small towns keep few secrets. The next morning when Mary drew water from the village well, did she overhear a toxic conversation from other women about Jesus? Were wives of the religious leaders chatting while filling water buckets? Were they rationalizing their husbands' assault on Jesus? Sadly, Mary realized that the sword of malice had been unsheathed.

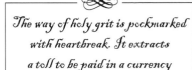

The way of holy grit is pockmarked with heartbreak. It extracts a toll to be paid in a currency of sorrow and suffering.

The scurrilous vitriol continued. It followed Jesus to Jerusalem, where he disputed the Pharisees by revealing the darkness they embraced. Proud professors of moral supremacy do not easily accept correction. They hurled rebuttals challenging his credibility. He claimed that the truth would set them free.[23] They countered that they were not slaves in need of freedom because Abraham was their father. Furthermore, they vilified Jesus as someone "illegitimate," a term for a person born from fornication. John Piper noted that their criticism was not veiled. They were labeling Jesus as obscene.[24]

We have no record to indicate that Mary heard this, but we are left with room to wonder if the heartbreaking news trickled back to her. The Gospels certainly document that the calumny toward Jesus intensified. Furthermore, merchants who traveled from Galilee to Judah selling their products and produce in Jerusalem would pass along whispers of information upon their return to Nazareth. Word-of-mouth news would eventually spread to Mary.

If a sword to pierce her soul was unsheathed by the hatred and rejection of her son, it was sharpened and readied by his arrest and trial. A plan designed by religious leaders to capture Jesus needed an insider to betray him.[25] The half-light of Gethsemane served as the point of attack, and a disciple volunteered to identify Jesus to the Temple guard and Roman soldiers. When Mary heard that Judas betrayed her son, did she ask why it had to be a friend? Did she comprehend that "only a friend can betray a friend, a stranger has nothing to gain, and only a friend comes close enough to ever cause so much pain?"[26]

The Gospels don't tell us where Mary stayed that night. She was in Jerusalem for the celebration of Passover and probably stayed with friends or relatives. Did a frightened disciple inform her about the arrest of Jesus? Did she learn the next morning that He had been interrogated by the past and present high priests, Annas and Caiphas? I have often wondered if Mary stood inconspicuously in the crowd when Pilate shouted, "Behold, the man!"[27] Could she see that Jesus's face was swollen? Did she notice that He winced in pain when the guards pulled His arm and slapped His back? Mary must have heard the raucous crowd stirred by religious leaders bellowing, "Crucify him!"[28] A chant as unimaginable in horror as it was unendurable in her ears. A thousand disturbing questions whirled inside her.

She followed Jesus to Golgotha. John's gospel account indicates that she was standing by the cross. How does a mother watch her son writhe in pain while impaled on a cross gasping for air? Her courage to remain and bear that heart-crushing agony astounds me. Helpless but unwavering, Mary remained close by as the sword of Simeon's prophesies plunged painfully into her soul.

In forty-five years of pastoral ministry, I have watched too many mothers lose their sons and daughters to death's cold grip. I have listened to their canyon-deep sobs. I have felt their aching grief when whispering "goodbye." I have walked beside them, leaving a hospital trauma room as they shuffled outside to a vehicle that whisked them back home to an empty room that moaned with gloom.

Mary heard her son's last words. Jesus tenderly exhorted her to embrace John, the beloved disciple, as her son. He told John to care for her as his mother. Before John escorted Mary away, she likely heard a triumphant cry through Jesus' parched lips. "It is finished," he declared with unmistakable conviction. His redemptive sacrifice was completely accomplished.

In those final moments on Golgotha, I wonder if Mary understood Jesus' anguished cry. Did the brutality of trauma choke her faith? Did she comprehend that instead of resignation, Jesus voiced a triumphant affirmation? He completed the redemptive sacrifice for our sins. He had never sinned, but He became sin on our behalf so that through Him we might be made right with God.[29] John escorted Mary away and down the craggy slope of skull hill. Afternoon shadows stretched dark fingers over Jerusalem. A shy disciple named Joseph received Pilate's permission to remove Jesus from the cross. Nicodemus helped Joseph as they meticulously cleaned Jesus' body and wrapped it with strips of linen. They used over seventy-five pounds of gummy myrrh and aloe mixture to glue the strips together.[30] Did Mary join her friends from Galilee who watched as Jesus was placed in Joseph's tomb?[31]

A forlorn Friday morphed into a long, silent Sabbath that yielded an unexpected Sunday. At dawn, some women who went to the tomb excitedly returned to tell John and Peter that it was empty.

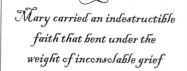

Mary carried an indestructible faith that bent under the weight of inconsolable grief but it never broke.

Breathlessly, they tried to explain the angel's statement that Jesus had risen. John raced Peter to the tomb. They found it empty except for the linen wrappings. John knew he needed to tell Mary so that impossible heartbreak could give way to irresistible hope. The truths Mary treasured in her heart across the years resurfaced from the depths of grief. She inhaled the air of indescribable joy! Jesus had risen just like He promised!

Weeks later, Mary joined the disciples in the upper room, faithfully obeying Jesus' command to wait for the promise of the Holy Spirit. Neither the gospels nor other books in the New Testament canon make mention of Mary again.[32] She was the first person to sing about her Savior.[33] And we can be reasonably assured that she was among that group of believers on Pentecost to testify that Jesus was the resurrected and reigning Savior.

So what makes Mary such a striking example of holy grit? Among her many sterling qualities, I believe it was her perseverance that stands out most magnetically. Despite daunting impossibilities that would crush most of us, Mary carried an indestructible faith that bent under the weight of inconsolable grief. But it never broke. Tim Perry agrees. He states in his book *Mary for Evangelicals*, "What sets Mary apart from us is…her perseverance. After a lifetime of wrestling with ambiguity, beginning at the manger, continuing through the temple encounter, and coming to a climax during Jesus' ministry, Mary is numbered among the first disciples in the upper room, awaiting the promise of the Father."[34] Holy grit can be a variegated virtue. It can be speckled with rugged audacity like Paul or flecked with serene strength like Mary. Consequently, she is proof that ironclad grit mixes well with velvet tender grace.

Gritty Take Aways

- **"Anyway moments" can reveal a lot about your faith.** How you respond to seemingly impossible situations can be a tipping point leading to a breakthrough of trust or a breakdown of hope. Punctuating your "anyway" moments with an exclamation of obedience to God can make a supreme difference.

- **Effective parenting requires a gutsy and godly resolve.** Courage is a premium virtue because tough decisions have to be made. Modeling holy grit as a parent involves pleasure and reward on one hand and exhaustion and pain on the other.

- **Your path of holy grit is never divorced from heartbreak.** Heartbreak can occur without holy grit, but holy grit will eventually and necessarily include heartbreak. God allows us to face debilitating grief to strengthen our devotion to Him. Mary's example can stir us to persevere through our tribulation because God expects us to take giant steps of surrender as she did.

CHAPTER 6

Truth is so obscure in these times, and falsehood so established, that unless we love the truth, we cannot know it.

Blaise Pascal

O death, where is your victory? O death, where is your sting?

I Cor. 15:55 ESV

Our doubts are traitors And make us lose the good we might win By fearing to attempt.

William Shakespeare

John the Baptist: Staying the Course of Truth

People in the village called him a fool. They thought he had lost his mind. He sold his trio of goats to buy a hammer, a chisel, and a crowbar so he could move a mountain. Yes, a mountain that stood between his village and the nearest hospital forty-three miles away.

Dashrath Manjhi was an impoverished laborer living in the Bihar region of India, where the Himalayan Mountains pose against a faint skyline in distant Nepal. When Manjhi's wife died from injuries sustained during a fall from a mountain trail, he decided to make a way through the mountain. He started hacking, striking, picking, and digging. By day he held down a job plowing fields. By night he chipped away at a proud mountain.

Villagers shook their heads scornfully as they watched. Manjhi's father joined them and ridiculed his effort. The temperature during the summer season could exceed 100 degrees, and with the sweltering heat came torrential thunderstorms that soaked the ground and drenched his spirit. Still, he continued day after day, week after week, year after passing year. A man of less determination would have stopped after five or six years. Manjhi relentlessly stayed the course until he had carved a corridor through the mountain that was 360' long, 30' wide, and 25' high. He began in 1960 and completed the task in 1982 to provide his village with closer access to medical care. He gave twenty-two years of his life to be a "way maker" and shortened the distance from forty-three miles to less than ten miles. The man so many people considered eccentric made a way where there had been no way. He earned the moniker "The Mountain Man" and carved a path of hope for others.[1]

Does that kind of perseverance inspire you? It challenges me to the marrow of my bones. It compels me to ask what price of commitment am I willing to pay to achieve a goal that may not come to fruition for two decades. It prompts me to consider what kind of pathway I can make despite long and painful years. What protracted endurance can I provide for broken people to experience the healing grace of Christ?

Twenty centuries before Manjhi, an original way maker emerged on the stage of history. His name was John, and he earned the moniker "the Baptizer" because he challenged people to repent and demonstrate their change through public baptism. A mountain of religious rituals blocked him. Hearts made hard by long years of pride and prejudice stood in the way. With a hammer of truth, a chisel of courage, and a crowbar of the Spirit, John cleared the way for the Messiah.

Among the titans of holy grit, John the Baptist cannot be overlooked. If there had been billboards in the wilderness of Judea promoting extreme devotion, the rugged face of John would have been featured front and center. He personified the word steadfast. He modeled persistence. He lived simply and serenely. He spoke fearlessly. He preached boldly. Most importantly, he stayed the course of truth and pointed others to the Lamb of God.

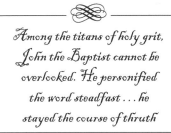

Among the titans of holy grit, John the Baptist cannot be overlooked. He personified the word steadfast . . . he stayed the course of thruth

Living with Missional Discipline

One of the reasons we have such meager information about John's formative years lies in his supporting role. He was not the main attraction. He stated emphatically that his role was secondary to that of the Messiah. His entire life and ministry were driven toward a brief consuming mission of pointing others to Jesus.

John was the only child of godly parents. His mother, Elizabeth, was a descendant of Aaron. His father, Zechariah, was a priest in the division of Abijah.[2] The angel Gabriel declared that John would embrace the discipline of abstinence from wine and liquor, but he would be full of the Holy Spirit. Furthermore, with zeal like Elijah the prophet, John would turn the hearts of fathers back to their children and prepare people to listen to the Messiah's message of salvation.

John was destined to be a man of holy grit. He grew up in a devout home that practiced self-discipline. His father instructed him in Scripture. The custom of Hebrew tradition involved memorization and recitation of the Torah beginning at age six.

John was familiar with the priestly duties of his father. Duties that involved preparing and performing sacrificial rites, caring for ritual items, maintaining and teaching the institution of covenant, adjudicating cases involving temple matters, announcing atonement for sins, and examining and purifying lepers.

The silent years between John's childhood and his adult ministry were preparatory years instead of empty ones. We don't know what skills he developed or what kind of work he did. We don't know if he stayed close by to help his aging parents or if they died, leaving John alone as a teenager.

After the discovery of the Dead Sea Scrolls in 1947, some scholars claimed that John might have been adopted by the Essenes into the Qumran Community because of his ascetic diet and his practice of baptism. The claim, however, is more speculative than it is convincing. Luke's gospel informs us that John grew up and became strong and lived in the wilderness.[3] John was radical before radical became popular. He learned the value of simplicity and solitude in the rugged outback, alone with God.

Solitude doesn't seem to be an appealing practice today. We binge on noise. We glut ourselves with activity. Researchers indicate that we consult our smartphones eighty times a day, nearly 30,000 times a year, "producing a welter of distractions" that split our focus and impede our concentration.[4] Busyness is our pet thief. We allow it to steal hours from the clock of significance. It pilfers contentment by demanding perpetual activity. We avoid serious introspection. We casually dismiss the lament of William Wordsworth, who said, "The world is too much with us . . . we have given our hearts away."[5] If the old poet were alive today, he would be traumatized to see how much more the world is with us and how easily our hearts have been seduced by hurry and impulse.

Henry David Thoreau observed that the majority of people in his New England world were absorbed by trivialities and delusions. He determined to find the core of life in the solitude of nature. He built a small cabin on the edge of Walden Pond in Concord, Massachusetts. There he lived alone in simplicity for

> *Busyness is our pet thief.*
> *We allow it to steal hours*
> *from the clock of significance.*
> *It pilfers contentment by*
> *demanding perpetual activity.*

two years. In his own words, he said, "I went to the woods because I wished to live deliberately, to front only the essential facts of life, and see if I could not learn what it had to teach, and not when I came to die, discover that I had not lived. I did not wish to live what was not life, living is so dear."[6] Thoreau didn't want to miss the essence of life but I think he misplaced his focus.

I think he misplaced his focus. He gave his attention to nature with far more energy than he did to the God who created nature. The woods of Walden afforded him valuable reflections about living, but solitude for the sake of solitude is an insufficient mission for life. Perhaps that's one reason Thoreau left Walden and decided to reconnect with life in Concord. Solitude without a mission can lead to isolation that starves the soul. A mission without discipline is like a ship without a rudder. Discipline enables us to reach a destination despite contrary winds and currents.

Solitude is not a merit that coerces God. It can be a discipline, however, that humbles us. We can't earn God's approval by utilizing solitude, but we can learn to listen to His voice when we mute the incessant clamor around us.

When we spend time in solitude with God, we pull away from the distractions that too easily capture us. We learn to look deeply inside and evaluate our thoughts and actions according to His standard. The reason solitude is a spiritual discipline is that it takes holy grit to stay the course of truth and continue life's mission. "The way to a deeper knowledge of God," wrote Tozer, "is through the lonely valleys of soul poverty and the abnegation of all things."[7]

John's solitude was shaped by a divine mission in a Judean wilderness. He caught and ate his own food, which consisted primarily of locusts and honey.[8] Some interpreters claim that the locusts John ate should be translated as "carob pods," but that claim lacks linguistic evidence. The Bible consistently regards locusts as insects. A swarming plague of carob pods would hardly frighten anyone or destroy their crops. Health experts indicate that locusts are highly nutritious and are still eaten in many parts of the Middle East and Africa. Locusts were also an approved food source according to Jewish dietary regulations.[9]

Furthermore, John dressed simply in a camel hair tunic accented with a leather belt. Both his diet and attire reflected a missional discipline that would challenge "the values of our society even more than it did his own."[10] John would have been considered unrefined

A mission without discipline is like a ship without a rudder. Discipline enables us to reach a destination despite contrary winds and currents.

and rough around the edges. He would not be warmly welcomed in a stiff and stuffy church. In the tradition of the prophet Elijah, John drew his strength from intimacy with God. Calvin Miller described such intimacy as an experience of sitting at a "wilderness table for two where lovers meet in the lonely desert of the human heart."[11] Indeed, we guard our intimacy with God best when we allow nothing to come between us and Him. Intimacy is a battleground where conflict erupts because we strip ourselves of self with serious difficulty. We do not like revealing to God the ugly places of our envy and conceit. We try to conceal our smug spiritual complacency as if it was something God did not know.

Like the boy Eustace in *The Voyage of the Dawn Treader*, we face a complicated challenge undressing. Eustace turned into a fierce and terrible dragon but soon discovered he wanted to be a boy again. He longed to undo what he had become. He tried to strip himself of scaly dragon skin, only to find another dragon skin beneath the old one. He was hopeless until he allowed Aslan, the Christ figure, to undress him. Only because of Aslan could Eustace get rid of the dragon skin and become a boy again.[12] We can only undress so far. We are not capable of complete restoration on our own. Only Christ can peel away our depraved scaly sin when we surrender what is in us to all He desires for us.

John impresses me as someone who offered to God all that was inside him. A rare surrender, don't you agree? Most of us are afraid that full surrender is a bridge too far. We hold back. We donate to God the painless things that we can afford to put on the altar. But holy grit allows no shortcuts to spiritual maturity. John gave God his best. His best devotion was shaped in a barren countryside. He spent his days praying and roaming the hardscrabble landscape carved by sharp ravines between mountain slopes. He spent nights sleeping beneath God's inexhaustible sky, meditating on scripture he had memorized. Hundreds of days and nights passed as John worshiped and patiently waited for God's signal to proclaim the Messiah. He surrendered his deepest desires and cherished ambitions to God's mission.

We misread John, however, if we think of him as a monastic hermit. Alexander Whyte, a venerable nineteenth-century Bible expositor, described John as a terrifying man not to be approached.[13] I disagree. A man like John, who lived so close to the heart of God, would fondly draw people seeking the light of truth even if he hammered those clinging to the darkness of deceit.

Despite spending much of his life in the wilderness, John made his way into Jerusalem three times a year to attend one of the feasts required of every Jewish male.[14]

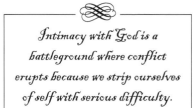

Intimacy with God is a battleground where conflict erupts because we strip ourselves of self with serious difficulty.

During those occasions, he reconnected with friends and made his sacrificial offerings. Although not a socialite, John could converse as easily with powerful individuals as he could with the humble and weak. Nevertheless, he likely made his way back to the wilderness as soon as possible. A missional discipline grounded John in a rich communion with God. A holy grit equipped him to stay the course of truth, communicating God's message regardless of adverse circumstances.

Communicating with Humble Boldness

John the Baptist thundered a message of repentance. He drew his authority from God. He challenged hearers to be baptized as an outward sign of an inward change. He was "a man sent from God."[15] When religious leaders asked about his identity, he quoted Isaiah the prophet saying, "I am a voice of one crying in the wilderness, 'make straight the way of the Lord.'"[16]

John didn't follow the cultural script of identity verification. It was customary to identify yourself by a job, a title, or a family. Sounds like the way we do it today. Not John. He identified himself as a voice for the Lord. Basically John was saying, "Who I am is not important. It's not about me. It's about the kingdom of God."

John declined to call himself a prophet, but Jesus declared that John was more than a prophet.[17] He felt unworthy to remove Jesus' sandals,[18] but Jesus testified that John was the greatest of men.[19]

In what way was John greater than others? Although John's personal qualities and his missional discipline were superlative, they did not make him greater. John's greatness was identified by an assignment that no other person had fulfilled. He was allowed to see, to know, and to testify about the Messiah whom all other prophets across the centuries had written and spoken about.[20] His greatness lay with the sacred message he preached in the unfolding purposes of God.[21] He was the link between the old covenant and the new kingdom. He preached with humble boldness to prepare the hearts of men and women to embrace Jesus.

You might wonder what role holy grit plays in preaching and why it's important. First, it plays an essential role because all biblical preaching communicated with clarity and grace will draw opposition. Whether the opposition is significant or inconsequential, a preacher must demonstrate holy grit through the situation. Second, it plays a key role because when opposition stirs in a congregation, a preacher must not quail before critics by diluting the purity of God's truth. He must stand serenely like the Reformation stalwart Martin Luther and prove that his "conscience is captive to the Word of God."[22]

Phillips Brooks knew something about preaching and holy grit when he stated, "If you are afraid of men and a slave to their opinion, go and do something else . . . But do not keep on all your life preaching sermons which shall say not what God sent you to declare, but what they hire you to say."[23]

Similarly, Billy Graham recognized the value of holy grit in preaching when he was wrestling with the prospect of speaking at England's prestigious Cambridge University. A sense of inadequacy overwhelmed him. He felt unqualified to preach in one of the intellectual capitals of the world. Graham was ready to cancel the event until an evangelical bishop with a Cambridge degree sent him a brief encouragement letter. "I can well understand your feelings of apprehension about Cambridge," the bishop wrote, "but Billy, do not worry.... Do not regard these men as 'intellectuals.' Appeal to their conscience. They are sinners needing a Savior. Conviction of sin, not intellectual persuasion, is the need."[24] Graham experienced a fresh affirmation and followed through with his meeting at Cambridge.

As a result of his perseverance, 400 students committed their lives to Christ.[25]

The preaching of John the Baptist glows with three unmistakable qualities. First, he was emphatically Christ exalting. John lifted high the flag of supremacy regarding Jesus as the Christ. His preaching burned with passion and kindled a flame in the hearts of people as they anticipated the Messiah. First-century Jewish historian Flavius Josephus noted that the crowds that heard John were deeply stirred and persuaded.[26] John unashamedly preached that Jesus was "The Lamb of God."[27] That title quickly resonated with Jewish listeners who were familiar with a lamb's role in the forgiveness of sins. John declared that Jesus was the Lamb of God "who takes away the sin of the world."[28] Furthermore, John proclaimed that Jesus was the "Son of God."[29]

Such a proclamation was no mere euphemism. John announced Jesus' deity as "the Son of God" because no mere mortal is capable of removing and forgiving sin. Jesus is not "a" son of God as if He was one among many. He was and is "the" sole and exclusive Son of God.

Second, John's preaching carried a bold, ethical demand. He communicated the absolute necessity of repentance. John stressed that turning to Christ involved turning from self-righteousness. Contrary to a contemporary idea that regards repentance as a change of opinion, John preached that it was a change of mind that leads to a change of life. He played no favorites and spared no fools. With vivid metaphors and courageous intensity, he rebuked, exhorted, and challenged listeners.[30]

When the Pharisees and Sadducees came for baptism, he called them "a brood of vipers" who spread poison like serpents in a garden.[31] He told them to show the fruit of repentance and stop leaning on Abraham.[32] Religious heritage couldn't earn them points with God.

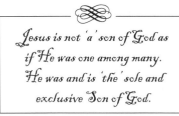

Jesus is not 'a' son of God as if He was one among many. He was and is 'the' sole and exclusive Son of God.

When people asked John how to live out the ethical demand of repentance, he pointed to the cruciality of compassion. He said whoever has two tunics should share one, and whoever has food should share with those who have none. When tax collectors asked how they should live, John instructed them to be honest and to collect only the amount of tax they were ordered to collect. When Roman soldiers asked him what they should do, he told them not to steal money by force, to stop making false allegations, and to start being content.[33]

Was John's style of communication too fierce and forceful? Would he even be allowed to speak in a church today? Critics claim that John was too much gristle and too little flavor. Admittedly, preaching that is void of warmth and wooing can repel rather than attract listeners. Moreover, preaching that demands a change of life without emphasizing the good news about a Savior who changes lives is not the gospel. We must understand, however, that John's role assigned by God required an "in-your-face" style to shake religious people out of their lethargy and awaken them to the reality of Christ.

After decades of preaching in a variety of settings, I've found that people will accept hard truth more often than they will listen to oral drivel. Dietrich Bonhoeffer, who communicated truth in the face of Hitler's tyranny, wisely warned that "nothing can be more cruel than the tenderness that consigns another to his sin (and) nothing can be more compassionate than the severe rebuke that calls a brother back from the path of sin."[34] Compassionate warning beats pious blabber every day! Holy grit reminds us that it is better to swallow bitter bold truth than to digest sweet bogus rhetoric.

The third quality of John's preaching relates to his joyful humility. He knew his limitation and celebrated the role he was given. He realized his message was preparatory,

Holy grit reminds us that it is better to swallow bitter bold truth than to digest sweet bogus rhetoric.

but Jesus' message was redemptory. When Jesus came to be baptized, John felt unworthy and requested that Jesus baptize him instead. He submitted respectfully when Jesus explained that His example of baptism was meant to "fulfill all righteousness." [35]

Later, when John's disciples jealously informed him that Jesus was baptizing and everyone was going to Him, John stayed his course. He refused the bait of envy. He replied, "A man can receive nothing unless it has been given him from heaven."[36] He reaffirmed that God was in charge. His trust in God's sovereignty dispelled any resentment about the fading status of his own ministry.

John displayed a sterling example of holy grit when it was time to play a backup position. "Second fiddle" is an idiom drawn from the world of music. Early orchestras often featured a musician who played the lead of the first violin. Another violinist playing a less prominent role became known as the "second fiddle." It morphed into a common expression for someone in a supportive and auxiliary role. John played second fiddle admirably with joy and humility.

Are you challenged like I am by the way John made so much about Jesus and so little about himself? He enabled the joyful music of the gospel to reverberate in the hearts of others. Second-fiddle ministry is often overlooked and seldom applauded. It serves in the shadow of others. Second fiddle is not second best in God's eyes. He sees it and He rewards it appropriately. If God calls you to play a backup position on His team, do it wholeheartedly. Don't complain. Don't covet a prominent position. Use your second fiddle for sweet harmony in the Kingdom orchestra, just as John did.

I was a guest speaker during a four-day event at a large church when a wealthy member asked if he could take me to lunch and discuss some theological issues. I realized early in our lunch conversation that his frustration had little to do with

If God calls on you to play a backup position on His team, do it wholeheartedly. Don't complain.

theology and everything to do with his young pastor. I listened to his litany of complaints for several minutes until he took a breath and asked my opinion. I sensed he might not like my answer, but I said, "You have a choice, sir. You can either be your pastor's worst nightmare or you can be his best encourager. Which choice do you think would honor Jesus and His church the best?" He stared at me for several seconds and replied, "I am the CEO of a prominent apparel company. I am not accustomed to such a straightforward reprimand, but I will evaluate your counsel."

A year later, the pastor told me how the church was thriving and how the CEO decided to be a phenomenal encourager, humbly serving behind the scene and ministering as a backup on every mission endeavor. John the Baptist was delighted to humbly back up Jesus. He insisted that he was not the groom at a wedding. He was the best man rejoicing over the groom.[37] When John stated, "He (Jesus) must increase, but I must decrease," he was not submitting an unwilling resignation.[38] He was giving a remarkable testimony of glad surrender. He personified holy grit at its finest! The statement, "He must increase, but I must decrease" is the most profound maxim of a Christ-centered ministry. It should be front and center in the heart of every follower of Christ. The problem for many of us is that we want Jesus to increase, but only if our status can increase too. A fixation upon self while trying to fixate upon Jesus is contradictory. The way for Jesus to increase is for self to decrease. When we fight Him for control of life's steering wheel, we inevitably cause a wreck and end up in a ditch of misery. The years of solitude in the wilderness with God taught John how to yield to God all the ambitions of his life and ministry.

The years with God also taught him how and when to get out of the way. John fulfilled God's purpose for his life. He stayed the course of truth. As the twilight of his ministry emerged, the ministry of the Son of Righteousness increased.

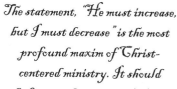

The statement, "He must increase, but I must decrease" is the most profound maxim of Christ-centered ministry. It should be front and center in the heart of every follower of Christ.

Dying with Blessed Assurance

He dazzled the strongest linebackers in pro football with his explosive power and shifty moves. He darted, juked, and swirled like a graceful gazelle ahead of hungry lions. Walter Payton and snarling opponents were always engaged in a savage fight for dominance on a football field. By the time he retired, he had rewritten several records in the NFL and earned a place in the prestigious Hall of Fame as one of the greatest running backs in history. Sadly, Payton contracted a rare liver disease and met the Pale Horse of death galloping toward him by the time he was 45 years old. Never afraid of a linebacker, Payton admitted he was afraid of dying. Robert Brazile, a close friend and former college teammate, said, "He told me he was scared. I never heard him utter those words before."[39]

Death rides toward each of us. Saying, "I don't want to think about it," won't make it go away. It's scary. Let's be honest and admit it. The last time I checked, the statistics on death were certain and conclusive: one out of one. The recent Covid pandemic claimed the lives of young and old across the globe and raised the fear of death to unprecedented levels. But death has long been feared and dreaded.

No one is exempt. Death strikes famous and powerful individuals just as it strikes the unknown and undone. King Louis XIV of France holds the title of the longest-reigning monarch in world history. He ruled for seventy-two years, but as he lay dying, he said to his son, "Profit from my errors and remember this: Kings die like other men."[40] Indeed, Kings, Queens, Presidents, Prime Ministers, and Shahs all die.

I wonder what thoughts of death meandered through the mind of John the Baptist while he languished in Herod's prison. I wonder if John ever heard a Latin proverb *veritas odium parit* popularized by a Roman playwright named Terence. It means "truth produces hatred." John lived truth and proclaimed truth. When he spoke truth about Herod Antipas' immoral life, John was whisked off to prison. Antipas hated that John said his marriage to Herodias was an unlawful adulterous disgrace. Herodias hated it more. She nursed a grudge and calculated revenge against John.[41]

Scholarly opinion varies regarding the place where John was imprisoned and the length of time he remained there. According to Josephus, Herod Antipas incarcerated John at Macherus.[42] Originally, Macherus served as a hilltop fortress on the east side of the Dead Sea, about fifteen miles from the mouth of the Jordan River. Antipas' father, Herod the Great, renovated it and transformed it into a gorgeous palace with a prison in the basement. However, Tiberias was the capital of Galilee. It was founded by Antipas, who named it in honor of the Roman Emperor Tiberius. The town featured impressive streets designed in Roman grid patterns at right angles with numerous shops. Antipas built a lavish public bathhouse fed by hot springs and a large stadium bordering the Sea of Galilee. He also built a magnificent palace where he resided. Several scholars contend that John was imprisoned in Tiberias because Macherus was nearly eighty miles away. Admittedly a royal banquet arranged for Galilean officials would seem reasonable in Tiberias where Herod Antipas and Herodias lived.

The length of time John remained in prison is debatable. Opinions vary from a few months to two years, long enough by either time to induce mental, spiritual, and physical trauma. I have a friend who served time in Mississippi's Parchman Penitentiary as a teenager. The Lord has strategically transformed his life. I have listened to him tell how incarceration works on the mind. How violence hardens the soul. How fear chills the heart. "There is also a dark loneliness that defies explanation," he says.

Perhaps you can identify with my friend. You sense the bars of incarceration around you too. Not physical bars but spiritual and emotional ones., The obstruction is real. You feel a heaviness in your soul that's hard to admit to yourself. The Lord seems distant. Doubt plunders your faith. The worship that once stirred your heart for Jesus has become stale. Your belief in goodness crumbles. You might not realize it, but you're not alone. Millions of followers of Christ have felt the same way you do.

So did John the Baptist. Can you close your eyes and picture him? The man that Jesus labeled as "the greatest" has slumped against a cold stone wall in a stench-filled cell. His zeal that once scorched religious leaders is gone. Disillusioned, he slinks down the wall to sit. He pulls his knees to his chest and wraps his brawny arms around his legs to stay warm. The dark loneliness that defies explanation prods him to send for his few remaining disciples. Can you hear the wound in his voice as he says, "please find out." He pauses, takes a deep breath, then continues, "find out from Jesus if He is truly the expected Savior or should we look for someone else?"[43]

John's anguish was a cry for assurance. Haven't you felt that in your moments of anguish too? We all need a blessed assurance when we are locked in despair and pleading for hope.

> We all need blessed assurance when we are locked in despair and pleading for hope.

When I was a young pastor living the dream of being married to the love of my life and basking in the joy of being a daddy to a beautiful little girl and a brilliant little boy, I sat in a room waiting for a medical report. I was stunned to hear a hematologist speak the word "leukemia" to me. He said further tests were needed. I drove home trying to process the bad news. I told my wife and we both cried. Later that night, when she and our children were asleep, I devoured chunks of truth from God's Word, especially the Psalms. I prayed passionately. I begged for God's intervention. I asked for the courage to embrace the hard stuff. Somehow on that sleep-deprived night, I decided to surrender a worst-case scenario to the Lord. I found a pen and wrote a free verse poem as my "Reply to Death."

> *We shall meet one unsuspecting day*
> *Or could it be that old and worn*
> *I'll be waiting for you.*
> *Either way, you cannot keep me*
> *For another bought me by His grace*
> *And He alone knows when and where*
> *The meeting will take place*
> *That sets me free for what*
> *He calls eternity.*

John needed a reply to death. He needed to hear from Jesus. Herod Antipas and Herodias were planning a banquet. Herodias was orchestrating the details so that the final entrée would be a severed head on a platter.

We should commend John for sending his doubt and impatience to Jesus. We often cloak our doubts in secrecy and hide our impatience behind a guarded smile. It is significant that in the squalor of his dismal situation, John entrusted his frustration and confusion to Jesus.

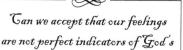

Can we accept that our feelings are not perfect indicators of God's presence or God's purpose?

Let's pause right here. Let's ask ourselves these thorny questions. Are we willing to entrust to Jesus our doubts and frustration? Can we confess, "Lord, I'm confused and impatient with my situation? I know that your answer might not be what

I want. Nevertheless, I entrust it to you?" Can we pray, "Lord, the dungeon of doubt where I'm confined is debilitating? It's so very hard. If it gets harder, you are still good, and I'll endure the worst?" Can we admit that our suffering has meaning even if it makes no sense at all? Can we accept that our feelings are not perfect indicators of God's presence or God's purpose?[44]

When our children were small they would run to our bedroom during a stormy night with blankets and pillows in tow. One night when thunder rattled the windows and jagged bolts of lightning surrounded us, I heard the pitter-patter of small feet. Then a soft thud on the carpeted floor beside our bed as they lay down. After a few minutes, I sensed a small hand lightly tapping the bedcovers in search of me. "Daddy, are you here?" my daughter asked. Drowsily I replied, "Yes, I'm here." After another booming clap of thunder, frantic little fingers furiously hunted for my arm. "Daddy, I can't feel you. Are you really here?" she complained. Now reason with me. From my daughter's perspective, her inability to feel my presence was an indicator of my absence. However, based on my presence, her feelings were unreliable. In case you're wondering, I did drop my arm off the side of the bed to hold her hand and calm her anxiety. My whole point is that although our feelings can run the spectrum of our emotions, we can't rely on them as substitutes for faith.

The eyes of our soul are often myopic until we see a distant truth more clearly.

When Jesus received the question from John's disciples, His reply exceeded a simple "yes." John needed something more than an intellectual explanation. He needed a definitive demonstration that Jesus was the expected Messiah. The eyes of our soul are often myopic until we see a distant truth more clearly.

To the question, "Are you the One?" Jesus replied with a revelation of "Watch what I do." For John's sake, Jesus illustrated the prophecy of Isaiah. He instructed the troubled disciples to tell John what they saw and heard: "the blind receive their sight, the lame walk, lepers are cleansed and the deaf hear; the dead are raised up and the poor have good news preached to them."[45]

The image of that moment when John's disciples returned with a message is saturated with anticipation. John rises from the floor of his cell and shuffles toward them, eager to hear what Jesus said. A slow smile moves across his bearded face as expectation swells in his heart. He wants to latch upon every sentence. A disciple begins, "John, this is what Jesus wants you to realize."

- *The blind who stumbled in perpetual darkness are gazing at sunsets and laughing with their children.*
- *The crippled have sold their mats at the market and have taken up jogging in the fields of Galilee.*
- *The lepers have learned to dance, and they delight to show off their healed hands and feet.*
- *The deaf rise early to hear the doves coo, and they stay up late listening to the owl's hoot.*
- *The dead walk in the villages, happily talking about the grand miracle.*
- *Better still, the poor have reserved seating wherever I proclaim the good news.*

The message satisfied John. It was a sacred confirmation preparing him for an executioner's axe. Herodias did not tolerate truth from a prophet. The party she orchestrated thrilled Herod Antipas. Especially when Herodias' daughter performed a provocative dance stirring Antipas to make a rash vow granting whatever she wished. After conversing with her mother, she wanted John's head on a platter immediately. Consequently, Antipas obliged her immediately.

John heard the clomp of soldiers marching toward his cell. An executioner read John the verdict. He neither flinched nor resisted. The forerunner had completed his mission. He died with a blessed assurance that he had stayed the course of truth.

What are you doing with the mission Jesus has given you? Have you allowed your discipline to atrophy? Has worry slowed you to a stop? We all make daily decisions that affect our momentum.

Find a place right now where you can read God's Word without distraction. Take a sheet of paper and write about your failures and struggles. Then pray and ask for fresh courage to stay the course of truth. Don't be surprised if you see the clouds of confusion fading away and the light of perseverance breaking through.

Gritty Take Always

- **Staying the course of truth requires missional discipline.** A mission without discipline is a ship without a rudder. Building intimacy with God requires time and solitude. Holy grit allows no shortcuts to spiritual maturity. When you allow the Lord to strip away the sin of busyness and selfishness, you are equipped to resist the peril of distractions.

- **Humble boldness is a crucial factor in communicating God's truth.** Don't lower the flag of Jesus' supremacy when you testify about Him. If God requires you to play a backup position, do it wholeheartedly. Don't complain. Second fiddle is not second best in God's eyes. Always keep this maxim at the core of your life and work: "Jesus must increase, but I must decrease."

- **You need to prepare for how you will reply to death.** Your feelings can trick you. They are not perfect indicators of God's presence or God's purpose. The blessed assurance you need is found by trusting Jesus to guide you through seasons of doubt and confusion.

CHAPTER 7

It is important for us to remind each other and ourselves that putting shame to death, as in crucifixion, is a slow process, and we are partnering with God as its executioners.

Curt Thompson

Therefore there is now no condemnation for those who are in Christ Jesus.

Romans 8:1 ESV

God does not define us by the worst thing we ever did. Jesus makes amazing use of flawed disciples. He continually invites us back, forgives us, and restores us.

Adam Hamilton

Peter: Prevailing Against Shame

Why is it that some people are better known for one failure than for all their successful accomplishments? Did Shakespeare capture a common sentiment when he wrote, "The evil that men do lives after them. The good is oft interred with their bones."[1] Epic failures and infamous feats seem to resonate longer and settle deeper into our memory. We tend to maximize deeds of debacle and minimize acts of virtue.

Roberto grew up in Buenos Aires where he channeled his athleticism toward golf. As a young teen, he caddied for other golfers and taught himself to play. He went on to become a world-renowned professional golfer winning tournaments in South America, The United States, and Europe, including a two-stroke victory over Jack Nicklaus in the 1967 Open Championship at Royal Liverpool, England.

He might have won the 1968 Masters Tournament, too, had it not been for an error with a pencil on a scorecard. Roberto fired a 65 on the final day, tying Bob Goalby for the lead. A playoff looked certain. Professional golfers are required by the rules of the Professional Golf Association (PGA) to keep an opponent's scorecard as well as their own. At the conclusion of a match, both players must review the accuracy of their score and place their signature on the scorecard. Once a player signs his scorecard, it stands as the official score.

Roberto's playing partner and opponent on that final day at the Masters was Tommy Aaron. After Roberto carded a birdie 3 on the 17th hole, Aaron accidentally wrote down a par 4. When Roberto reviewed his scorecard, he hastily signed it without realizing that Aaron had written down a final score of 66 instead of the actual score of 65. Aaron admitted the mistake and apologized for it, but the rules committee chairman informed Roberto De

Vicenzo that the card he signed was official. Consequently, he was the runner-up, and Bob Goalby was declared the winner.[2]

Roberto's mistake became legendary. For all his victories around the globe, he is usually remembered for his fateful faux pas in the 1968 Masters at Augusta National Golf Club. One of sport's greatest ironies is that one of golf's most successful players is best known for his failure.

Colossal mistakes and horrendous failures can happen to any of us. But the moniker of shame hangs heavier upon the neck of some individuals more than others. Shame can be an emotional vampire sucking faith out of the soul. It can bleed hope from the mind and deplete love from the heart. Brene' Brown claims that shame is something everyone experiences because it "tends to lurk in all the familiar places, including appearance and body image, family, parenting, money and work, health, addiction, sex, aging, and religion. To feel shame is to be human."[3]

Shame can be a powerful internal voice telling us we don't count, we are not enough, and we never measure up. It is a strong feeling that we are hopelessly different and beneath the standard of appropriate

> *Shame can be an emotional vampire sucking faith out of the soul. It can bleed hope from the mind and deplete love from the heart.*

human behavior.[4] Shame sends a message into the core of our being that we are unacceptable, worthless, and deplorable.

Guilt and shame are close relatives, but there is a crucial difference. Guilt declares that we "did" something wrong, whereas shame declares that we "are" something wrong. Shame is a crafty and condemnatory tool. It is a favorite weapon of Satan who is called "the Accuser." (Rev. 12:10)

I first felt the burden of shame in connection with asthma. From elementary school through high school, I battled it. I missed a lot of school days. Medical treatments that are common today, were not readily available back then. I grew accustomed to emergency room visits and oxygen tents. It might have been easy for elementary-grade classmates to conclude that I was simply embarrassed about my asthma. If so, that was a false assumption. I knew well the blushed feeling of embarrassment. It occurred when my teacher interrupted my daydreams as I stared out a window and my friends giggled. Asthma was not a mere embarrassment. It shamed me. It accused me in sports activities. It tortured me during social events.

I remember a sixth-grade field trip. As I took my seat on the bus, everyone was giddy with excitement. I began struggling to breathe. A well-intentioned girl told the teacher that I had asthma again. She emphasized the word "again" loudly and slowly. Another friend tapped my shoulder and asked, "Hey, you're not going to ruin our trip, are you?" My teacher didn't know what to do. She thought I needed cough syrup. She tried to console me saying, "Just try to breathe like normal people." I wished I could more than she could imagine.

Once the bus began moving, I hoped someone would open a window. I was wheezing heavily and gasping for breath, but the bus driver didn't allow open windows. When we made our first stop, my classmates scampered out of the bus. When I shuffled past the driver, he heard my wheezing and asked in a gruff voice, "What's wrong with you, boy?" I saw his frown. The word "wrong" cut deeply. Nobody else in the class was "wrong" like me. Shame overwhelmed me. Soon my teacher called the principal to request that I be sent home. Later that evening my parents took me to the ER.

During the summer of that same year, I excelled at baseball. I played shortstop and pitcher on a Little League team. One sultry June evening an asthma attack struck when I was on the pitcher's mound. I labored to breathe. Between pitches, I bent over, putting my hands on my knees to draw deeper breaths. I tried to pretend that I was okay. The assistant coach trotted to the mound. His long sigh expressed his disappointment: "Okay, we're gonna need someone else to pitch. You ought to find out what's wrong with you, son." There was that word "wrong" again. I was disappointing to him. I was "wrong" because I was unable to finish pitching. I was the problem. Shame won regardless of the score.

With all the friction shame causes in our souls, it would seem to be something that we could summarily discard. Shame is slippery, however. It morphs and hides. It waits until the opportune moment to unleash its denunciation. My struggle against shame was minor compared to the shame I've heard from other followers of Christ. It taunts them wherever they go. Even on good days, the shadow of shame can creep over them as they strive to mute the internal podcast of condemnation.

Holy grit is effective against shame because the battle is protracted. Shame can erupt at any time and flare-up in unexpected ways. It's not a once-and-done fight. The battle requires relentless perseverance.

Have you been lugging a backpack of heavy shame? If you haven't found a healing place where you can release your shame, I hope that by the time you read the last page of

In the hushed attic of night when the Accuser starts tossing around musty crates of shameful memories and opening boxes of failure from your past, it's crucial to reach for the nail scarred hands of Jesus.

this chapter, you will discover God's liberating grace and inhale the sweet air of His acceptance. I pray that you will discover, in the hushed attic of night when the Accuser starts tossing around musty crates of shameful memories and opening boxes of failures from your past, that it's crucial to reach for the nail-scarred hands of Jesus.

In nearly every survey of favorite Bible characters, Simon Peter is consistently near the top. I identify with him because I share his weaknesses, but I admire him because of his strengths. In some strange way, his impulsive personality, his habit of speaking before thinking, and his boast that he would not deny Jesus endear him to me. Here's a question I have tossed to believers over the years: Do you suppose Simon Peter battled shame about his denial of Jesus? If so, how did he recover? Track with me and let's explore a side of holy grit that deals with shame and delights with recovery.

An Unforgettable Failure

I live with an unforgettable failure. No, it's not indecent but it still haunts me. When it happened, I had been a pastor for twenty-five years and I had officiated more than 150 weddings. The wedding that remains so unforgettable is the one I forgot. Well, almost. Here's how it unraveled. I had counseled a young couple and looked forward to the Saturday afternoon when I would perform their wedding ceremony. I genuinely loved that couple and I think they loved me. Anyway, a few days before their big day, the wedding coordinator informed me that it would not be necessary for me to attend the rehearsal. She said, "I'll tell them that you will lead them through their vows and the exchange of rings. I'll also explain how you will conclude by challenging them to love each other deeply and live large for Jesus." It sounded great to me. After all, wedding rehearsals can be exceedingly boring.

On the morning of their wedding day, my wife, Sharon, assigned me the task of digging large holes to plant azalea and loropetalum bushes. I finished after a couple of hours, took a lunch break, and decided to mow the lawn. At nearly 2:00 that afternoon, Sharon dashed out of the house into the yard and yelled in a voice of panic, "Honey, you have a wedding in five minutes! The coordinator just called and wondered if you remembered." Suddenly, I did! I was sweaty and dirty. With minimal traffic, we lived twenty minutes from the church if we caught green lights. During heavy traffic with stops at every red light it could take thirty minutes. I replied. "Tell the wedding coordinator that I'm coming and tell her to instruct the pianist and orchestra to play everything they know."

I set a personal record for a shower and shave. Sharon said, "I'll drive. You can dress in the car." I grabbed my suit, shirt, tie, socks, and shoes and jumped into the passenger side, hoping I wouldn't appear obscene in my t-shirt and boxer briefs as we left our neighborhood.

I was slipping on my pants when Sharon stopped at a traffic light. A man in a truck beside us glanced at me in disgust. Cars just aren't suitable for dressing. The light turned green. I prayed as Sharon raced toward the church, skidding into the parking lot. I vaulted out of the car, ran past an usher at the entrance, and saw the groom standing beside the double doors of the worship center. I looked to see if he was holding a knife or a gun. I started to apologize, but he interrupted by hugging me and exclaiming, "Pastor, we thought you had been hurt in an accident." I told him it was worse than that. I had forgotten!

In a moment, we stood at the altar waiting for his bride's entrance. No one in the audience seemed happy to see me since I was forty minutes late. I noticed the bride's mother on the second row. I couldn't blame her for giving me the stink eye. I worried she might lift her hand and slide it sideways under her chin making the "cut your throat" sign. Soon enough, the ceremony was over. I felt lower than a snail's belly. Some friends suggested I should remain that low. John David smirked and shook his head. "How in the world can you forget a wedding?" he asked. "Apparently it's easy," I contended. "You just start working in your yard on a hot August day and the heat evaporates your memory."

News spreads quickly when you forget a wedding. The following week a couple in our church told me they were moving to Texas to live closer to their grandchildren. The wife thanked me for being their pastor and affectionately said, "We will always remember you." Her husband chuckled and added, "Yeah, how could we forget the pastor who forgot a wedding?"

Thankfully, my unforgettable failure has a shelf life. In seventy years, no one will be around to recall it. Now consider Simon Peter's failure. It was unforgettably recorded in the Gospels so that every person who ever read Matthew, Mark, Luke, or John would read about his denial of Jesus.

How would you like it if your most vile sin against Jesus was published and preserved so it would be known to every future generation ad infinitum? What would you feel if every time your name was mentioned it was attached to your despicable denial of the Savior?

Peter was the point man among the disciples. He was the leader of the band of brothers. The courageous captain of the Carpenter's team. Among the disciples, no one spoke to Jesus more often than Peter. In turn, Jesus spoke more often to Peter than to any other disciple. When Jesus met him, He tagged him with the nickname "Cephas," meaning "stone" or "rock." There is an anticipatory emphasis in that moniker. Jesus looked beyond who and what

Following Jesus at a distance is a prelude to failure. We grow cowardly by distance. We grow fearless by intimacy.

Peter was at that moment to affirm who and what he could become. The first and last command that Jesus gave to Peter was the imperative "follow Me."[5] Sprinkled between those two imperatives lay many ups and downs and a few bold assertions like, "If they all fall away from you, I will never fall away," and "Even if I must die with you I will not deny You."[6] Peter's sincerity was not the problem. His self-confident pride and his inability to comprehend the frailty of his flesh was the big problem.

After a detachment of Roman soldiers accompanied by Jewish officials arrested Jesus, he was taken to the palace of Caiaphas, the high priest. Peter followed at a distance and found a fire pit in the courtyard to warm himself.[7] The phrase "followed at a distance" represents something more than a simple description. It indicates spiritual vacillation. Following Jesus at a distance is a prelude to failure. We grow cowardly by distance. We grow fearless by intimacy. How sadly odd that the man who defended Jesus with a sword earlier that evening would hear a question from a young girl that sent him into a blatant renunciation. Not once, but three times, Peter denied any knowledge of, or any association with, Jesus. The third denial was laced with an outburst of profanity.

The sound of a rooster crowing pierced the darkness. In the palace archway, perhaps fifty or sixty feet away, Jesus stood looking at Peter. The Greek word translated as "look" refers to a direct and intentional gaze.[8] The look was not one of angry condemnation. It was a look of wounded compassion. Have you known that "look" from Jesus? I have seen it in my own moments of denial. In his book, *A Fragile Stone: The Emotional Life of Simon Peter,* Michael Card wisely notes that if we read about Peter's heartbreaking failure, but our own hearts don't break, then we have failed to interact with the details of Scripture.[9] Peter knew his failure all too well, and it was unforgettably burned into his conscience. He quickly left the courtyard weeping and shattered over his sin.

A Heavy Shame

Some sounds remain with us for the duration of life. Researchers inform us that our memory for things we've heard is less reliable than our memory for things we've seen and touched. But a sound associated with a defining experience finds a file cabinet in our brain where recall comes quickly whenever the sound reoccurs. I imagine the sound of a rooster's crow piqued Peter's memory many mornings after his denial of Jesus. Peter knew the sound of shame. He heard shame in the mob's angry voice shouting, "Crucify Him." Shame reverberated from the distant hammer blows on Golgotha's hill when rusty spikes impaled Jesus' wrists and feet on a cross. Shame resounded in the thunder as darkness enveloped a weepy sky over Jerusalem. Shame wouldn't allow Peter to ignore the memory of his boast. He had emphatically declared that he would never be disloyal. He said he would stand courageously with Jesus even if all other disciples cowered in fear. He would never back away or back down.

Peter's conscience begged for relief. Did he revisit better days of serving Jesus? Did he think about the moment when his brother Andrew excitedly introduced him to Jesus? Did he chase sunlit conversations with Jesus when they traveled from Galilee to Judah? Could he picture Jesus teaching the crowds and sharing parables of truth? Did he ponder Jesus' miracles and revisit the afternoon when the Lord took a boy's offering of five loaves and two fish to feed thousands?

Did Peter push against shame by reflecting on the tender way Jesus healed his mother-in-law or the stunning moment when Jesus brought the daughter of Jairus back to life? How could he dismiss from his mind the grandeur of Jesus' transfiguration? How could he forget that day near Caesarea Philippi when he affirmed that Jesus was the Christ, the Son of the living God?

Did a rooster crow at dawn on the first day of the week when Mary Magdalene claimed that Jesus' body had been removed from the tomb? Was Peter's mind flooded with confusion and anxiety when he and John found the tomb empty, just as Mary said? The heavy shame of his denial threatened to bury the good in his devotion.

Anyone who has ever battled shame can identify with Peter's struggle because:

- *Shame can be a thick fog clouding a clear view of faith.*
- *Shame can be a toxic inner critic vetoing hope.*
- *Shame can be a massive boulder blocking love.*
- *Shame can be a heavy anchor drowning joy.*

My friend Carlos carried a compelling personality. People were drawn to him like iron shavings to a magnet. He lit up a room when he entered. He could brighten a dark winter's day with his laughter. He treasured his wife and his little boys.

Carlos also lived with a heavy shame. He battled a drug addiction. It was a monster that he could not beat. The addiction crushed him and threw him into a pit of recrimination. He grew familiar with rehab centers and the cycle of failure, shame, detox, a year or two of sweet abstinence, then failure again. And shame again. The shame grew louder and stronger with every failure. I prayed with Carlos frequently. He genuinely loved Jesus, but he kept failing. Shame spoke the language of hopelessness. Shame said, "You are beyond help. Jesus couldn't love you." Shame told him to give up. Shame shouted, "Put an end to your pain. Your family is better off without you."

Tears still gather in my eyes as I tell you that Carlos listened to the voice of shame one Sunday morning and put a bullet through his chest. I was asked to speak at his graveside service. Preaching the funeral message for a friend can be hard. Preaching the funeral message for a friend that chose suicide can be the hardest.

A couple of hours before the service, I overheard the comment that "anyone who commits suicide goes straight to Hell." I knew I would need to address that opinion. So, I framed my words carefully as I stood at Carlos' graveside. I referred to the promises given in Romans 8:38-39 that "neither death nor life...nor anything else in all creation can separate us from the love of God in Christ Jesus our Lord." I explained that no one goes to Heaven because of the way they live, and no one goes to Hell because of the way they die. No one lives good enough to earn salvation, and no one dies bad enough to lose salvation. My friend didn't live perfectly, but he did place his faith in a perfect Savior who saves imperfect people who battle the shame that too often overwhelms them.

Recently, I baptized Carlos' twelve-year-old son. He honored his dad by wearing one of his dad's t-shirts into the baptismal pool. Joy drenched everyone who witnessed the baptism. Thanksgiving flooded my heart as grace conquered shame in that moment.

Surely, Peter deliberated over the warning Jesus gave about Satan's attack. Satan intended to sift Peter like wheat.[10] The process of sifting wheat was a common sight to Peter. It involved a vigorous tossing and crushing of the wheat in order to separate the grain from the chaff. Peter knew that Jesus referred to Satan as "the evil one," the "ruler of this world," "a murderer," and "the father of lies."[11] Satan's plan involved tossing the disciples into stagnation, separating their faith from Jesus, and crushing them into the dirt of Jerusalem. The diabolical nature of Satan

No one lives good enough to earn salvation and no one dies bad enough to lose salvation.

has not changed over the centuries. He still desires to sift followers of Christ today. His evil strategy continues. He intends to maim, murder, and malign those who place faith in Jesus as Lord. For those unwilling to trust Jesus, Satan is content to keep them enslaved.

I find it significant that years later, Peter challenged believers to realize that Satan is like a lion seeking to devour whoever he can. By resisting Satan and standing firm in the faith, his intimidating roar sounds more like a purring cat.[12] Satan is a supernatural enemy and he must be fought with supernatural weapons and a sufficient measure of holy grit. A heavy shame is a devastating explosive device in the Accuser's armory. With it he destroys millions of men and women.

Peter's shame was crippling, but he watered a mustard seed of faith in the crevice of his memory. Such a tiny kernel of hope was wrapped inside a fragile recollection about turning back to Jesus and strengthening other believers.[13]

Can you identify with Peter's failure and shame? Perhaps you've blown it, and you're wondering if you will ever have a renewed relationship with Jesus. Your memory

An unforgettable failure is never unforgivable. A hauntingly heavy shame is never unredeemable.

replays joy-saturated days when you danced in the sweetness of His approval. Somewhere along your journey, you found yourself gathering around enticing fire pits where sloth, lust, greed, anger, rivalry, and malice persuaded you to deny Jesus. When you did, a rooster crowed in your conscience and you couldn't shake the shame. You have a longing to turn back to Jesus. You want to help others do the same, but you doubt He could forgive such flagrant sin. The cure for shame begins when we return to Jesus in humble repentance and confess our failure. Confession is not merely an "oops" about our sin. The word "confess" in the New Testament means to speak the same, to agree, and be like-minded. So when we confess, we are speaking about our sin the same as Jesus says. We make no excuses. We agree with Him that we are sinful and wrong. In godly sorrow, we turn to Jesus and away from our sin so that the heavy shame is lifted and obliterated. An unforgettable failure is never unforgivable. A hauntingly heavy shame is never unredeemable.

I visited an eighty-six-year-old lady in the hospital. I knew her to be a gentle, loving, and faithful follower of Christ. She told me she wasn't afraid of dying, but she was worried that she hadn't been forgiven "enough" because of some shameful things in the days of her youth. In reply to my question about what she meant by "enough," she tearfully mentioned, "Well, what if there's something else I need to do?" I took her frail hand and knelt down on one knee beside her bed. I tenderly said, "Everything that needs to be done for your forgiveness has been done by Jesus at the cross. He did enough because you never ever could. He took the penalty for your sin so that by faith in Him you could stand forgiven before God." More tears flowed. She caught her breath and said, "Thank you for reminding me of that truth. Years and fears had almost made me forget it." When I left her room, I walked down the hospital corridor and silently prayed, "Lord, no matter how hard the years or how big the fears, grant me a holy grit to remember that you are always enough!"

A Healing Restoration

After Jesus' death and burial, Peter and six disciples went fishing one evening. I am convinced that they encountered a sensory overload. Everywhere on the Sea of Galilee, beneath a night sky alive with stars, Peter sensed something familiar: the faint whiff of tilapia spawning, the rhythmic sound of boat oars whooshing through the water, the coarse texture of the net between his fingers.

He also sensed something of Jesus. There, on the shore of Galilee, Jesus once borrowed Peter's boat for a teaching platform. There, Jesus miraculously filled the boat with an overflow of fish and he called Peter to follow Him. There, on the Sea of Galilee in the fourth watch of the night during a violent storm that threatened to drown the disciples, Jesus walked toward them. Did Peter feel again, if only for a second, the rush of his once breathtaking faith when he stepped out of the boat and toddled on the water toward Jesus?

Throughout the night and into dawn's first light, Peter chased a thousand moments with the Savior he so deeply loved but so shamefully denied. If he longed to jettison the infamy in his soul and reconnect with Jesus, the opportunity arrived when John, peering through an early morning fog, shouted ecstatically, "It is the Lord!"[14] Peter wasted no time grabbing his cloak and plunging into the water. He swam eagerly to shore, leaving John and the other disciples the task of bringing in a net spilling over with fish. He stood dripping wet, looking at Jesus. He noticed the fish and bread on a charcoal fire that evoked fresh memories. Like the day when Jesus multiplied the fish and bread to feed five thousand seekers. Like the night when he stood by a charcoal fire and denied Jesus. Peter knew intuitively there was an unresolved problem, and Jesus would not allow Peter to dismiss it.

Prevailing against shame requires us to place it at the feet of Jesus. A healing restoration demands an honest and clear facing of our failure.[15] When a night of denial turns into a guilty morning, we need a restoration. When a season of arrogant pride leaves us desperate for holy cleansing, we need a restoration.

Peter's restoration began when Jesus asked, "Do you love me

more than all of these? [16] Three times Peter had denounced that he knew Jesus, much less loved Him, and three times Jesus asked Peter the same question, "Do you love me?"

What did Jesus mean by "more than these"? Was he referring to the other disciples? Or was he referring to Peter's vocation of fishing? Good arguments can be made for either answer. Peter did claim to love Jesus more than any of the other disciples. Consequently, Jesus may have been urging Peter to confess that his love was not, in fact, greater than the rest of the disciples. On the other hand, Peter's entire life revolved around fishing. Therefore, Jesus may have been prompting him to decide between a love for a life-long vocation and a love for a life-changing Savior.

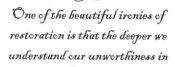

One of the beautiful ironies of restoration is that the deeper we understand our unworthiness in the light of Jesus' grace, the more intense our love for Him grows.

Truth is found in both answers because Jesus expected Peter to exercise a love greater than he ever had loved. Much has been made about Jesus using a different Greek word for love than Peter used. Jesus used the verb "agapas," while Peter replied with the verb "philo."[17] Both words, however, are used throughout the New Testament to express God's sacrificial love as well as the love of believers toward one another. Although the two words are often synonymous, there can be a nuanced difference when they are used close together in the same verse.[18] Perhaps Jesus chose the word "agapas" because it conveyed a sacrificial love more than the word "philo," which typically conveyed a friendship love. Most likely, however, the variation in the words is less significant than the emphatic declaration of genuine love above everything else. Leon Morris explained in his study of love in the Bible that the supreme question between Peter and Jesus was the question of love.[19]

Teaching, preaching, evangelism, vision casting, and leadership take secondary place to the all-consuming importance of love. Spiritual gifts are valuable, but love is vital![20] Jesus wanted Peter to love Him and, consequently, to love people like He did. Peter needed to be mastered by Jesus' love, so that he could effectively minister in Jesus' love.

Peter could no longer boast that he loved Jesus more than his friends did. Humility replaced bravado. He confessed that Jesus alone knew the measure of his love. A healing restoration never bypasses contrition and brokenness. One of the beautiful ironies of restoration is that the deeper we

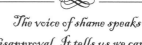

The voice of shame speaks disapproval. It tells us we cannot be valued by Jesus. The voice of grace speaks acceptance. It tells us that we are the Savior's beloved.

understand our unworthiness in light of Jesus's grace, the more intense our love for Him grows. We understand more acutely that love covers a multitude of sins.

Windows of hope opened in Peter's soul as Jesus gave him a commission after each question. The shame that could hinder Peter's service is the shame that can denounce our service also. Thousands of believers today are not serving Jesus because they have listened to the wrong voice. The voice of shame speaks disapproval. It tells us we cannot be valued by Jesus. The voice of grace speaks acceptance. It tells us that we are the Savior's beloved. He welcomes our repentance. He delights to use us again in His service. The choice is crucial. We can obey the voice of shame or we can obey the Savior who removes shame.

The antitoxin for shame is always the grace of God through Christ. Grace is God's healing of our unworthiness. It is His embrace of our unacceptable behavior and undeniable sin. I have often thought that the adjective "outrageous" should be used to describe God's grace. Obviously, it is "amazing," as John Newton avowed, but it is also "outrageous" because it turns conventional thinking upside down. By the term "outrageous," I'm referring to something shocking. To accept someone who does not deserve acceptance disrupts our sense of fairness. It stuns our logic like holding a fork in an electric socket zaps our hand. To forgive someone who can do absolutely nothing to make forgiveness warranted can seem like a miscarriage of justice. Such criticism of God's grace and forgiveness is not a recent charge, however. Celsus, a caustic second-century critic of early Christianity, scornfully asked why God held such a "preference for sinners".[21] Origen, a Christ-centered theologian in that day, refuted Celsus and explained that God's preference for sinners existed so that through Christ they might be converted. God's loving grace toward shame-shrouded sinners is outrageously redemptive. He receives the broken and hopeless, the popular elites, the unpopular deplorables, the wretched reprobates, the miserable moralists, as well as the famous and the infamous. His grace provides a seat of forgiveness at the table of restoration.

Mike Gillich was both famous and infamous. He owned a popular nightclub and an erotic dance lounge in Biloxi, Mississippi. He was a kingpin in a criminal organization known as the Dixie Mafia. Gillich emerged into national prominence when the FBI implicated him in the murder of Judge Vincent Sherry and his wife, Margaret. Gillich was convicted and given a fifteen-year sentence for his conspiracy in their murders. While Gillich was serving his time, my friend Billy Hanberry was ministering in a facility where Gillich was incarcerated. The two of them gradually developed a friendship. Billy talked often about the forgiveness and grace of Christ, but Gillich was dismissive. The shame of a notorious life and plotting the death of a beloved and respected couple weighed heavy. Several years passed until one day, Billy pressed Gillich to decide if he was going to reject Christ and wallow in shame or if he wanted to surrender his sinful life to the only Savior who could remove his guilt. Gillich stared at Billy. Then slowly bowed his head and humbly begged Jesus to forgive him and take over his life.

A few days later, Billy called to ask if I would baptize Mike Gillich. I wasn't sure that I heard Billy clearly, so I asked him to repeat his question. He explained that Gillich had listened to me preach on TV a decade earlier, and he wanted me to baptize him.

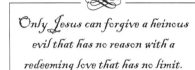

Only Jesus can forgive a heinous evil that has no reason with a redeeming love that has no limit.

I remember meeting Mike Gillich as I stood beside a baptism pool. He looked frail. Gone was the swagger that accentuated his profile. I held his hand as he gingerly stepped into the water. A man that had been known as a cold-hearted criminal declared his faith in Christ and slipped beneath the water, giving testimony of a changed life. Some people wondered if Gillich's conversion was genuine. I think it was. I hope it was. Gillich died a few years later. He had lived with a horrible memory, but he died with an outrageous grace. Only Jesus can forgive a heinous evil that has no reason with a redeeming love that has no limit.

In a similar way, Simon Peter experienced an outrageous and overflowing grace that ignited a fresh fire of devotion. Jesus challenged Peter to feed and lead believers: to feed them God's truth and to lead them in Kingdom service. In concert with Peter's restoration, Jesus also issued a sober prophecy about what awaited him. Peter must have known that the statement, "you will stretch out your hands" [21] referred to crucifixion.[22] He would follow His

Savior and glorify God in his death by crucifixion. Peter didn't object. He didn't plead for an easy way to avoid the cross. After all, since Jesus had conquered the grave, Peter could face it. He would faithfully "follow in His steps."[23]

Of course, The Book of Acts tells us the rest of Peter's story. He boldly proclaimed the message of the Gospel during Pentecost without the chains of shame holding him back. Three thousand new believers entered the kingdom. When night fell and Peter reclined on his bed, I imagine he sensed the smile of His Savior. Perhaps the Spirit whispered into his soul, "keep on prevailing against shame. The crowing of the rooster is over. Practice holy grit and spread the Gospel."

I treasure individuals who have been permanently scarred by Jesus' forgiveness. They know the fire of grace that burned away the malignancy of sin. They move forward by faith but look back only to see how far they have grown beyond shame.

Peter's final written words are recorded in his second epistle. They could serve as an epitaph for his life: "But grow in grace and knowledge of our Lord and Savior Jesus Christ. To Him be the glory both now and to the day of eternity. Amen."[24] The shame that threatened to dominate Peter's memoir became an asterisk. Jesus' grace rewrote his story.

Have you settled the shame factor in your life? Standing against shame requires a truckload of holy grit. But rejoice and go forward! God's grace is infinitely greater than all your shame.

Gritty Take Always

- **Shame can be a merciless enemy warring against your soul.** It is a devastating explosive device in the Accuser's armory. Shame is a powerful internal voice telling you that you don't count, that you are not enough, and that you never measure up. Shame is not quickly or easily defeated. One of the reasons holy grit is vital against shame lies in the nature of the battle. It is not a one-and-done fight. The battle against shame requires relentless tenacity.

- **God's Word assures you that unforgettable failures are not unforgivable.** The cure for shame begins when we return to Jesus in humble repentance and confess our failure to Him. Satan desires to sift followers of Christ today. He intends to maim, murder, and malign anyone who trusts Christ. By resisting Satan and standing firm in our faith, his intimidating roar sounds more like a purring cat.

- **Prevailing against shame requires you to place it at the feet of Jesus.** A healing restoration demands a clear facing of our failure and a contrite acceptance of our Savior's outrageous forgiveness. The voice of shame speaks disapproval. It tells you that you cannot be valued by Jesus. The voice of grace speaks acceptance. It declares that you are the Savior's beloved. You have a choice. You can go through life obeying the voice of shame, or you can obey Christ who removes shame. Trust Christ and move forward in holy grit.

CHAPTER 8

*What is under our skin, and under
the skin problem in America, is
a spiritual problem . . .When we
focus on another person's skin, we
miss the reality of our own sin.*

Benjamin Watson

*But whoever hates his brother is in the
darkness and walks in the darkness and
does not know where he is going because
the darkness has blinded his eyes.*

I John 2:11 ESV

*No one ever said that a battle would be
easy...But there is one truth we can take
comfort in knowing, and that is that we
have not been asked to fight this battle
alone. We have a Coach, and He has
a strategy - a kingdom strategy - His
kingdom agenda. He has guaranteed us
victory if we will only play by His book.*

Tony Evans

ul: Combating the Sin of Racism

te for holy grit is urgently needed in the battle against racism. I carry childhood memories of shameful racial disparity. I remember sitting with my mother in the lobby of a doctor's office as an eight-year-old. I wondered why there were two water fountains. Above one fountain was the inscription "colored." Above the other was the inscription "white." I remember the school desegregation era in South Georgia. I saw the anxiety on the faces of black students. I heard the scurrilous comments and racist words. I desired to make friends with the new black students but listened to the lie that black kids didn't want white friends. Mistrust and doubt stalked the hallways of the school. Misinformation reigned until courtesy and kindness took root.

As I look back on that troubling time, I grieve. I cannot fully comprehend the hurt and pain that my African American brothers and sisters experienced. I am unable to fathom the despicable history of

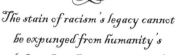

The stain of racism's legacy cannot be expunged from humanity's ledger, but the continuation of its malice must not be condoned.

slavery and the Jim Crow atrocities of bias, bigotry, and brutality.[1] I have never heard the door of opportunity slammed shut against my children because of their skin color. I cannot imagine suffering from generational poverty.

I am fully aware that strongholds of racial superiority are not easily conquered. Walls of longstanding hatred do not fall quickly. Unregenerate human nature is hopelessly corrupt apart from the change that Jesus makes.

Cornelius Plantinga rightfully emphasized that the heart of sin refuses to take responsibility for its sin, and it rejects the painful way of repentance.[2] The stain of racism's legacy cannot be expunged from humanity's ledger, but the continuation of its malice must not be condoned. Jesus does not allow us the option of loving Him without loving others. If we have been reconciled to Him, we are obligated to be reconciled to others regardless of race or ethnicity.[3]

My purpose in this chapter of Holy Grit is not to offer a comprehensive history of racism. Others have detailed the sinful story of racism meticulously and in a manner far more effective than I could. I intend to expose its evil in light of God's Word through the ministry of Paul. Consequently, I want to apply biblical truth to relevant ideological issues behind racism.

The Culture Paul Inherited

We don't get to choose the culture into which we are born. When Paul took his first breath, he inhaled an air dominated by the influence and authority of the Roman Empire. The empire reached from "The shores of the English Channel in the north, to Egypt in the south, from the straits of Gibraltar in the west to Mesopotamia in the east."[4]

Paul's life began in Tarsus, the capital city in the Roman province of Cilicia, located in the northeastern corner of the Mediterranean. It was a prominent center of commerce, academia, and "philosophical indulgence."[5] Citizens of Tarsus avidly pursued education and learning in schools that rivaled Athens and Alexandria.[6] Tarsus gained fame for merchandising a soft long wool woven from goat hair called "cilicium." It was widely used for tents, sails, awnings, and cloaks.[7]

If we have been reconciled to Christ, we are obligated to be reconciled to others regardless of race or ethnicity.

Paul testified that he was born in Tarsus of the tribe of Benjamin, brought up in Jerusalem, educated under Gamaliel, nurtured as a Pharisee, and enjoyed Roman citizenship since birth.[8] He excelled in the two languages of Hebrew and Greek and likely had proficiency in Aramaic and Latin. He mastered the Torah and outstripped his contemporaries, expounding and defending the Law. He served as an enforcer for the Sanhedrin, tracking and arresting Jews who embraced Jesus as the Messiah. He approved the death of Stephen and guarded the coats of those who hurled the deadly stones.[9] Paul terrorized followers of Christ. His rage drove him to seek and apprehend men and women in Damascus, nearly 140 miles from Jerusalem. Along that journey, the Risen Lord interrupted and invaded Paul's life. His rebel will was profoundly transformed. Paul, the ruthless terminator, became Paul, the gospel communicator.

Jesus infused Paul's personality with a gritty passion and gave him a three-fold mission: (1) to be a servant and a witness to Jews and Gentiles, (2) to proclaim what he had experienced in his saving encounter, and (3) to embrace the promise of deliverance from adversaries he would face.[10]

As a Jew in the Pharisee tradition, Paul's keen grasp of the Old Testament and Hebrew tradition provided him the opportunity to connect with fellow Jews wherever he traveled. As a citizen of the Roman Empire, Paul was protected by the rule of law. He could travel freely anywhere within the broad stretch of the empire to declare the gospel message to Gentiles. Estimates vary, but there is solid evidence that Paul's travels on land and sea covered at least fifteen thousand miles.[11]

A good way to understand the culture in which Paul ministered is to highlight the socio-cultural aspects of daily life in the first century. Stay with me. This brief outline will provide a basic picture of the world Paul encountered and the grit he needed to spread the gospel in a prejudicial and discriminatory culture.

Roman society featured a hierarchy of social groups. The senatorial class consisting of approximately 600 members stood at the top.[12] Individuals in this group were quite wealthy. They held the highest legal positions and served as members of the Senate. Next stood the Equestrian class so named because they originally served as the royal cavalry. They were paid to purchase and care for their horses to facilitate trade and commerce. Later they became businessmen who amassed considerable sums of money. They filled many of the military and administrative roles in the empire. The Plebeians followed the Equestrians. This group represented the majority of individuals in the Roman Empire and served as Rome's working class. They were farmers, cooks, builders, and manual laborers.

Next stood the freedmen. They comprised a social sub-class of former slaves. They were granted freedom by their owners through a legal procedure called manumission. A freed slave of a Roman citizen was given citizenship and received privileges to earn money and advance to important civic positions.[13]

Last in the social ranking were slaves. Historians contend that slaves made up one-third of the population in urban areas throughout the empire.[14] Some estimates indicate that eighty five to nighty percent of the inhabitants of Rome and the peninsula of Italy were either slaves or of slave origin.[15]

The moral and spiritual carcinogens of prejudice, ethnocentrism, bias, partiality, and bigotry feed the cancer of racism whether in the first century or the twenty-first century.

Men and women became slaves in several ways: (1) by capture in war, (2) birth into a slave family, (3) through purchase,

165

(4) by kidnapping, (5) through debt to a creditor, (6) trade from human traffickers, or (7) by punishment for a serious crime.

Although some slaves were treated respectably and kindly by their owners, the vast majority of them were vulnerable to physical abuse and violence. Legally a slave could be flogged, starved, or crucified.

Ironically, slavery in the Roman Empire was based on "neither skin color nor ethnic racial origin."[16] The Romans secured their slaves in places throughout the Mediterranean world without consideration of skin color.[17] Tragically, the empire's socio-cultural structure was inseparably welded to slavery. Speaking against it required strong moral grit that often aroused animosity.

Although slavery in the first century was seldom based on a person's race, the seeds of racism were embedded in its heinous practice. The moral and spiritual carcinogens of prejudice, ethnocentrism, bias, partiality, and bigotry feed the cancer of racism whether in the first century or the twenty-first century.

Paul's Subversion of Racism

Some critics argue that Paul's message is at best inferior to Jesus' message and at worst antithetical to Jesus's teaching. I strongly disagree. I am convinced that Paul was so devoted to the message of Jesus as revealed in the gospels of Matthew, Mark, Luke, and John that if we lacked those documents, we would still be able to know the character, personality, and teachings of Jesus, as well as His crucifixion, resurrection and abiding presence. In other words, as Yale historian Kenneth Scott Latourette said, "If we were confined to Paul's letters we would not be led to a picture of Jesus essentially different from that which the Gospels give us." [18]

Without belaboring the point, there is plenty of evidence to support the unity of purpose and perspective between Jesus and

Paul. No one should doubt that Paul's message about salvation, forgiveness, reconciliation, harmony, respect, and compassion is welded to Jesus' truth.

When you examine Paul's letters to churches in various places where he preached, and when you examine his personal letter to Philemon, you can sense his grit as he uses the gospel to sever the roots of racism.

- **To Christians in Galatia**

   Paul's message to believers who lived in the region of Galatia blazed with certainty about the sole sufficiency of Christ. He declared that through Jesus alone there is forgiveness. Consequently, justification before God comes through His son and not through the Law of Moses. Neither the Jewish race nor the Jewish religion could atone for sin. Every person, regardless of skin color, nationality, or social status, is on the same level in need of God's grace. There is no room for arrogant pride or ethnic superiority.

   To emphasize that God shows no bias and that His gift of salvation is not based on race, Paul cited an incident with Peter at Antioch.[19] Peter was enjoying fellowship with Gentile followers of Christ until some Jewish leaders from Jerusalem arrived. He withdrew from the Gentiles to curry favor with his Jewish associates who believed that eating a meal with Gentiles would make them spiritually unclean. Peter's action influenced Barnabas and other Jewish Christians to alienate themselves from Gentile Christians. Paul publicly rebuked Peter. Their conflict was not a mere clash of personalities. Instead, it was an exceedingly theological issue as Timothy George points out.[20]

   God saves everyone on the same basis of grace through

faith in His son. Paul laid the axe of truth on the root of racism when he declared, "There is neither Jew nor Greek, there is neither slave nor free, there is no male and female, for you are one in Christ Jesus."[21]

Paul did not deny distinctions of ethnicity, social status, or male and female physical diversity. He simply, but profoundly, stated that none of

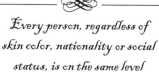

Every person, regardless of skin color, nationality or social status, is on the same level in need of God's grace.

these things should usurp the authority of Christ to cement believers into a unity of holy equality. Paul boldly stressed that Christ had established something new in a community of transformed people. Jews and Gentiles could sit down on the same level at the table of grace. Slaves and free persons could embrace one another as equals. Men and women could gladly humble themselves to fulfill their God-appointed roles with respect and support for one another. A community of crucified oneness could begin. A community that joyfully replaces coerced rules of ecumenity.

- **To Christians in Thessalonica** [22]

Paul's message to believers living in the bustling city of Thessalonica brimmed with affirmation and exhortation. He applauded their perseverance in the face of persecution, and he reminded them of their moral responsibility as followers of Christ. Specifically, he instructed them to repudiate vengeance and retaliation in favor of kindness and patience. Christ-like behavior cannot be overstated in the battle against racism. The tragic hypocrisy of claiming to be a follower of Christ but living in a way that distorts the gospel and demeans the dignity of others because of race is appalling and decisively unchristlike.

Frederick Douglass, the courageous abolitionist, wrote in his autobiography about the horrid inconsistencies he loathed in so-called Christians who practiced racism and supported slavery. He referred to the man who robbed him of hard-earned wages at the end of each week but met him as a leader on Sunday morning to show him the way of life and the path of salvation. He called out the religious advocate who sold black women into prostitution but campaigned for purity. He rebuked the pious churchman who proclaimed it a sacred duty to read the Bible but denied Douglass the right of learning to read the name of the God who created him.[23]

Christ-like behavior cannot be overstated in the battle against racism. The tragic hypocrisy of claiming to be a follower of Christ, but living in a way that distorts the gospel and demeans the dignity of others because of race is appalling and decisively unchristlike.

When Paul and Silas declared the gospel at Thessalonica, opponents accused them of turning the world upside down.[24] Don't you wish the evangelical churches in America could be accused of turning the world upside down with the liberating message of the gospel lived out magnetically by followers of Christ?

Don't you wish we could be accused of injecting the world with such love, peace, forgiveness, and reconciliation that racial animosity would be scarce rather than prolific?

169

- **To Christians in Corinth**

    Living for Jesus in Corinth required vigilance and perseverance. On three occasions, Paul reprimanded believers for attending events in pagan temples.[25] No doubt, some of them had frequented the temple of Aphrodite, where worshipers paid homage to the goddess of love. A majority of Christians living in and near Corinth came from a Gentile background that lacked the moral discipline of Judaism. Rivalry, divisiveness, sexual promiscuity, idolatry, superiority, and misuse of spiritual gifts characterized many believers.

    In addressing their situation, Paul focused on their identity in Christ and planted seeds of godly subversion that would, in time, lead to the demise of slavery.

> *Don't you wish we could be accused of injecting the world with such love, peace, forgiveness, and reconciliation that racial animosity would be scarce rather than prolific?*

    Was Paul supporting slavery when he wrote, "Were you a slave when called? Do not be concerned about it?"[26] Tragically, some early American slaveholders used this text to justify their racism. Their egregious mistake was based on a misinterpretation of the text and a violation of the context.

    Paul was not endorsing slavery for the obvious reason that the second part of that text states, "If you can gain your freedom, avail yourself of the opportunity."[27] Paul was referring to the Roman practice of "manumission." When slaves manumitted, their legal status changed to that of a freedman or freedwoman. Most slaves anticipated being manumitted into freedom by the time they reached thirty years of age.[28]

Paul contended that freedom was desirable, but freedom in Christ was paramount. Furthermore, Paul's exhortation, "do not become bondservants of men" (I Cor 7:23), is a clear indication that he did not view slavery as a suitable institutaion.[29]

Lisa Bowen's astute research in *African American Readings of Paul* underscores the way early African Americans utilized Paul's letters to combat racism. For example, Lemuel Haynes (1753-1833) was the first black man to be ordained by a religious organization in America. Haynes served as a minute man in the Continental Army during the Revolutionary War. He learned Latin and Greek and became the first African American to receive a college degree. Haynes challenged pro-slavery advocates and their interpretation of I Corinthians 7:21. He emphasized that although Paul lived in a culture of slavery, he never condoned it. Instead, Paul championed the right of every person to be free. Haynes further contended that God's edict of human liberty expressed in Paul's letters overruled the law of man that promoted slavery.[30]

- **Churches in Ephesus**

Ephesus was the capital city of the Roman province of Asia and one of the most prominent cities in the Empire. It featured a thriving commercial business as the convergence point of three heavily trafficked trade routes. Ephesus boasted an outdoor theater that could seat 25,000 spectators and took religious pride in its worship of cultic deities, especially at the Temple of Artemis (Diana), which was celebrated as one of the Seven Wonders of the Ancient World.[31]

Paul spent at least two and one-half years of ministry at Ephesus and addressed his letter to believers living in

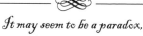

It may seem to be a paradox, but Christ created a whole new race that is raceless.

and around Ephesus while he was incarcerated in Rome. His message abounds with sacred doctrine and godly duty. He emphasized the necessity of unity in the church. Moreover, he urged believers to demonstrate a distinct behavior under the Lordship of Christ.

In Eph. 2:14, Paul explained that Jesus' atoning sacrifice on the cross abolished the "wall of hostility" separating Jews from Gentiles. The "wall of hostility" was a metaphor describing the barrier of Mosaic rules and regulations which separated the two groups. Jesus removed the hostility and secured peace by creating a new union. Through Him, all people have access to salvation by grace through faith. Inequality before God was removed because in Christ, we have been reconciled to Him and to one another. It may seem to be a paradox, but Christ created a whole new race that is raceless.[32]

Paul admonished believers to "be eager to maintain the unity of the Spirit in the bond of peace" (Eph 4:3). The importance of unity is obvious by the repetitive use of the word "one." In Eph 4:6-7, Paul emphasizes "One body, one Spirit, one hope, one Lord, one faith, one baptism, and one God and Father" over all peoples. Each person of the Trinity – Father, Son, and Holy Spirit calls for oneness that demonstrates a compassionate unity among followers of Christ. Since Jesus tore down barriers so that we could be reconciled to Him and to one another, shouldn't we advocate justice and speak up for the innocent?

- **A Message to Philemon**

Although Paul's message to Philemon is the shortest of his letters, it packs a strong appeal to God's redeeming grace as an antidote to the status of slavery and racism.

Many commentators have suggested that Onesimus was a runaway slave who stole money from Philemon, his master, and having fled to Rome, somehow found himself in prison with Paul. While that explanation is widely held, it is equally possible that Philemon sent Onesimus to Rome to minister to Paul, who was under house arrest. [33]

Paul may have led Onesimus to place his faith in Christ because he indicated that he "became his father" (v. 10). Consequently, Paul explained that he was sending Onesimus back to Philemon and urged Philemon to accept Onesimus on the basis of his new identity in Christ. Paul wanted Philemon to jettison the "slave and master" identity and embrace the "brother in Christ and partner in ministry" identity. By referring to Onesimus as a brother rather than a slave, it would indicate that Philemon accepted

Men and women transformed by Christ cannot maintain racial hostility and superiority over other men and women.

Onesimus into a relationship that invalidated the title of slave. Paul emphatically demonstrated to Philemon that he would take on the consequences of any wrongdoing if Onesimus was guilty of any offense.

This is the gospel in action. This represents the subversive power of the gospel to combat racism. Laws are often necessary to achieve justice. Laws, however, cannot change the human heart as Jesus can. A faith relationship with Him is the catalyst that explodes the enmity of racism. Men and women transformed by Christ cannot maintain racial hostility and superiority over other men and women. The new humanity marked by dignity, respect, love, forgiveness, and equality must be maintained.

Grit to Pursue Racial Harmony

Paul's determination to spread the Gospel throughout the Mediterranean region left a permanent impact on the Greco-Roman world. The message of redemption, repentance, and reconciliation took root in the lives of believers and bore fruit even in Caesar's houseold.[34]

Paul knew that the Gospel unleashed the power of God for salvation to anyone who put their faith in Jesus. The Greek word Paul used for power in Romans 1:16 is "dunamis." It is a word from which the English words dynamic, dynamo, and dynamite are derived. The Gospel serves as God's dynamite to explode racism, shatter hatred, and demolish racial superiority. Paul was the dynamo whom God appointed to proclaim that dynamic message. He boldly affirmed that all persons are image bearers of God's creation, and every person deserves respect and dignity. God shaped every man and woman from the one blood of Adam and He saves men and women by the one blood of His Son, our Savior.

As I write this chapter, racial tension is exceedingly high. Nearly a dozen American cities have erupted in protests or riots. Politicians point fingers of blame at one another, and community activists demand sweeping reforms in law enforcement. The road to racial reconciliation lies in need of constant repair. But, as

Miroslav Volf points out, "the human ability to agree on justice will never catch up with the human propensity to do injustice."[35] Nevertheless, we must pursue racial harmony

We must pursue racial harmony and not allow the clamor of culture or the politics of skin color to mute the voice of God's Word.

and not allow the clamor of culture or the politics of skin color to mute the voice of God's Word.

John Perkins is one of my heroes. His book *One Blood: Parting Words to the Church on Race and Love* should be required reading for every follower of Christ. John's story is written in blood. The blood that spilled from his broken body as a victim of racial rage and also the blood shed by Jesus that transformed John's life. For fifty years, he has been a compelling voice for racial reconciliation, forgiveness, and Christ-like love. John Perkins contends that "race is not a biblical way for us to relate to one another. There's only one race, but over time we've elevated things like skin color, hair texture, language, and ethnicity to a level where they become the main criteria we use to judge entire groups of people...This is wrong. This is a sin. But sadly, we've let it creep into our churches as well."[36]

Citing evidence from the Human Genome Project, theologian Wayne Grudem noted that while different physical traits such as skin and hair color can be identified between individuals, no consistent pattern of genes exists to distinguish one race from another. Furthermore, there is no genetic basis for the divisions of human ethnicity because the human genome sequence is 99.9 percent the same in all people.[37]

Any theory that persists in plunging the knife of retaliation into the wound of racism will never facilitate racial healing.

If there is only one race,

then where does the problem of racism lie? Does it lie with dermatology and the level of melanin in our skin? Does it lie with psychology and the emotional triggers of human behavior? Or does it lie with sociology and the social traits of people and institutions? Racism can infect and affect any of these disciplines, but the real problem lies elsewhere. It lies with hamartiology and the study of sin against God and one another. The destructive effect of sin is pervasive and entrenched in human nature. All of us are marred by sin and manipulated by its treachery. Tragically, our rationalizations and self-serving explanations about sin reveal the strength it holds on us. Extracting sin from our nature is impossible apart from the redeeming work of Christ who paid the price for our sin at the cross. As His followers, the quintessential question we must answer is: "What does the Word of God say to us about combating racism?" I am keenly aware of several theories that attempt to analyze and resolve the racism equation. My objection, however, is that some theories and some advocates subordinate the authority of Scripture to a preferred ideology that defines racism foremost as an institutional issue rather than a sin issue. Consequently, such theories propose retribution as the solution rather than redemption and reconciliation.

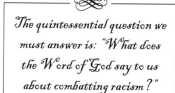

The quintessential question we must answer is: "What does the Word of God say to us about combatting racism?"

I am not implying that American institutions and agencies are faultless and undefiled by racism. I am contending that if the primary agenda of any theory is to fix blame then it will fail to fix the problem. I am pleading for sufficient intellectual honesty to recognize that any theory that persists in plunging the knife of retaliation into the wound of racism will never facilitate racial healing. Looking back and critiquing American forefathers because of their racial failure is appropriate. Expecting from them posthumous perfection, however, is an unrealistic standard no human can attain.

In *A Practical Guide to Culture,* John Stonestreet and Brett Kunkle offer wise counsel regarding three cultural lies about racism: Lie #1: "You are your ethnicity. Lie #2: Racism is nonexistent, so people need to get over it!" Lie #3: "Racism in the United States is happening everywhere all the time."[38] I would like to include one more: Lie #4: "Holy grit is powerless against racism." We cannot win the battle against racism by denying it exists, but we cannot overcome racism by refusing to persevere in the fight against it. As followers of Christ, we must not quit. We must speak up for truth and build up one another in love. If we let up and give up, then we cast reproach upon the message of the Gospel. Seeking justice is not an option, but any attempt to maximize social justice in a way that jeopardizes the supremacy of the Gospel is unacceptable. Thaddeus Williams hits the bullseye with his statement that "Instead of saying that social justice *is* the gospel or *in* the gospel, it is more helpful to say social justice is *from* the gospel."[39] When we make skin color our ideological magnum opus, we not only marginalize the Gospel, we disparage the worth of all skin colors. This is precisely the failure of the Critical Race Theory (CRT) because it selectively maximizes people of one skin color in order to disenfranchise people of different skin colors. Proponents of CRT view social interaction through the lens of hegemony and discrimination.

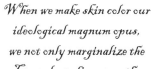

When we make skin color our ideological magnum opus, we not only marginalize the Gospel, we disparage the worth of all skin colors.

They blindly ignore the reality that past dominance and bias cannot be remedied by present and future prejudice in favor of preferential skin color.

The social justice pitch from CRT is like a moth that flutters and moves unpredictably in the name of diversity. God loves sacred diversity. He created the human race with immense diversity but unified by a shared profile as His image bearers. Ironically, the ideology of social justice in Critical Race Theory allows little place for human beings as individuals. "It reduces people to avatars or mouthpieces for the groups they belong to," argues Scott David Allen. They are expected to think and speak in conformity with everyone else in their group. Diversity is not tolerated.[40] Narrative agenda and groupthink are far more important than truth and evidence in CRT.

E. V. Hill served as Lead Pastor of Mount Zion Missionary Baptist Church in Los Angeles from 1961 until he died in 2003. Mount Zion was one of the largest African American churches in the nation during his ministry.

I treasured Pastor Hill's perspective on race relations and invited him to speak in a church I served. He had received scurrilous criticism from racist activists who tried to shame him for preaching about a 'white Christ.'

Pastor Hill weighed the criticism and replied, "I don't know anything about a 'white Christ' . . . I know about Christ, a Savior named Jesus. I don't know what color He is. He was born in brown Asia, He fled to black Africa, and He was in Heaven before the Gospel got to white Europe. So, I don't know what color He is. I do know one thing: if you bow at the altar with color on your mind and get up with color on your mind, go back again, and keep going back until you no longer look at His color, but at His greatness and His power – His power to save."

The Apostle Paul's admonition to the Ephesians is a holy grit mandate that is urgently applicable in the combat against racism. He wrote,

"Stand therefore having fastened the belt of truth and having put on the breastplate of righteousness, and as shoes for your feet, having put on the readiness given by the gospel of peace, In all circumstances take up the shield of faith, with which you can extinguish all the flaming darts of the evil one, and take the helmet of salvation, and the sword of the Spirit, which is the Word of God, praying at all times in the Spirit, with all prayer and supplication. To that end, keep alert with all perseverance making supplication for all the saints." (Eph. 6:14-18)

The words "perseverance" and "supplication" are powerful tools for holy grit. Vigilant endurance in the battle and steadfast prayer for one another must not be overlooked. If we persist in the Word of God, in truth, righteousness, peace, faith, salvation, and prayer, then we will nullify the echo chamber of racial superiority. During the middle years of the Civil Rights movement, Martin Luther King, Jr. sat in jail and wrote a sermon titled "Loving Your Enemies." The passing years have not diminished the impact of his powerful words: "Returning hate for hate multiplies hate, adding deeper darkness to a night already devoid of stars. Darkness cannot drive out darkness; only light can do that. Hate cannot drive out hate; only love can do that."[41] King's message reverberated the challenge Paul gave to believers living in Corinth. Especially the reminder that three things remain: "faith, hope and love,

> *If we persist in the Word of God, in truth, righteousness, peace, faith, salvation, and prayer, then we will nullify the echo chamber of racial superiority.*

but the greatest is love."[42] Followers of Christ are not only ambassadors, they are also agents of change and the love of Christ is the impetus.

I was Richard's pastor when he called one night to request prayer. For two years, he had suffered from congestive heart failure. His cardiologist had informed him, however, that within 48 hours he would receive a new heart. The transplant surgery was long and tedious. Thankfully, it was also flawless. After several months of healing, the elderly parents of the donor wanted to meet Richard. Joy and sadness drenched the occasion. One man's death made life possible for another man. Richard expressed his deep gratitude for the couple's son and a tender conversation followed. Then an awkward moment occurred. The couple asked, "Could we, uh... may we, uh... would you allow us to hear the heartbeat of our son, Joey?" They shyly confessed that they were infringing on Richard's privacy, but love compelled them to ask. They hoped Richard would roll back his shirt sleeve so they could put an ear on his wrist. He stared at them briefly. Then he slowly unbuttoned his shirt. His wife helped him lift his t-shirt. Tears flowed as both the mom and dad leaned over and placed their ear on Richard's chest. They listened to the thump, thump, thump that once belonged to their son. After regaining his composure, Richard made a statement to the donor's parents that I will remember forever. With intense conviction, he said, "I promise you that I will be the keeper of Joey's heart." Richard's story clings to my soul. It challenges me and humbles me to ask, "Am I a keeper of the heart of Christ?" Do I love and lead others the way He expects? Will others hear His heart when they listen to me apply scriptural truth in combatting racism?

Rejecting prejudice, partiality, and polarization requires the holy grit of love, acceptance, and forgiveness day by day.

Gritty Take Aways

- **Paul's letters clearly testify that every person, regardless of skin color, nationality, or social status, is on the same level in need of God's grace.** Because of the Gospel, every person is invited to repent of sin and place their faith in the atoning work of Christ and forge a community of crucified oneness. Men and women transformed by Him cannot maintain racial hostility and superiority over others.

- **Jesus abolished the wall of hostility between races and removed inequality for all who are reconciled to Him.** Laws are necessary and good to achieve justice, but laws are not able to change the human heart the way Jesus can. A faith relationship with Him is the catalyst that explodes the enmity of racism.

- **We must exercise holy grit in pursuit of racial harmony.** We must not allow cultural bias or the politics of skin color to mute the voice of God. Seeking justice is not an option, but attempts to maximize social justice in a way that jeopardizes the supremacy of the Gospel are unacceptable.

POSTSCRIPT

During decades of ministry, I have observed too many men and women who once burned with devotion for the Lord give up, cave in, bail out, and abandon their first love. The toll of time and tribulation overwhelmed them and they discontinued their journey of faith.

If you are sitting on the sideline too wounded and weary to go on, may I tenderly challenge you. It's not too late to re-engage. Before your story ends, what do you want it to say? What do you want your loved ones and friends to know? Before your final chapter is written, let your story speak of how you persevered. Let it tell how you crawled out of the pit and re-joined the company of the courageous.

In J.R.R. Tolkien's epic *Lord of the Rings trilogy*, there is a moment when Frodo admits that he can't continue. He is ready to give up and throw in the towel. His will to persevere is shattered. His friend Sam, who has experienced much of the same fatigue and fear, calmly tells him that their journey is like one of the great stories when people had lots of chances of turning back, only they didn't. They kept going because they were holding onto something. Frodo wearily asks, "What are we holding onto?" Sam replies, "That there's some good in this world, Mr. Frodo, and it's worth fighting for."

The good in your story and mine is the outrageous love and

grace of Christ who loved us and gave Himself for us. Holy grit is our gratitude offering to Him. It is the exercise of our will through agonizing seasons of waiting, forgiving, and enduring, modeled by Abraham, Joseph, and Caleb. Holy grit is our resistance against quitting, our trust during impossible moments, and our passion to stay the course of truth like Elijah, Mary, and John the Baptist. It means prevailing through dark nights of shame as Peter did and combating the sin of racism as Paul did.

I want to see you thrive. Don't let the last chapter of your story reveal that you took the easy exit for the road "more" traveled. I want to stand beside you one glorious ultimate day, knowing that as stewards of holy grit, we fought the good fight, finished the course, and kept the faith (2 Tim 4:7).

I'll leave you with this ancedote for your holy grit collection. When I was a boy growing up in South Georgia, I enjoyed playing with toy army men. Sometimes my friend Tommy and I would take the soldiers outside and position them in a large sand pit.

Tommy would take one platoon of toy soldiers and arrange them strategically for battle. I would do the same with my platoon. Then we would light firecrackers and engage in war. Now, if you grew up in an area where fireworks were prohibited, just stay with me. I promise we knew the power and the potential for harm. One hot July afternoon I was losing the battle. I had one soldier left, and he was perched on a rock about the size of a cantaloupe. We decided to take a lemonade break inside and later go back outside to finish. Tommy had six army men left when we returned. We each took a turn lighting a firecracker and tossing it toward a soldier. Amazingly I fought back until we each had one man left. Tommy decided to use his secret weapon – a "cherry bomb." A cherry bomb was a powerful round explosive the size of a small plum. It could shred a soft drink can. He tossed it right beside the rock on which my soldier stood. Sand and smoke flew up seven feet high. Neither the rock nor the soldier moved. Tommy conceded. "You win! I never could knock that soldier down," he groaned. "Do you know why?" I asked. Tommy shook his head. "When we went inside, I found the super glue, and when you were finishing your lemonade, I walked outside and glued my soldier to the rock."

That story has remained adhesive in my soul during hard times. Hopefully, it can remind you that when the world, the flesh, and the Devil blast you with danger, doubt, despair, deception, and disillusion, you can withstand it all if you just stay glued to the Rock of Salvation – Jesus Christ.

EPIGRAPH NOTES

Chapter 1: Abraham: Enduring a Severe Wait

1   Peter Marshall, <u>Mr. Jones, Meet the Master.</u> (New York: Fleming H. Revell, 1950), 189.
2   <u>Isiah 40:31</u> (NKJV).
3   Adelaide A. Pollard "Have Thine Own Way" <u>Baptist Hymnal</u>(Nashville: Convention Press, 1975), 349.

Chapter 2: Joseph: Finding a Way to Forgive

1   C. S. Lewis, <u>The Weight of Glory</u> (San Francisco: Harper Collins, 1949), 182.
2   Luke 17:3-4 (CSB).
3   Coretta Scott King, comp. <u>The Words of Martin Luther King, Jr.</u> (New York: Newmarket Press, 1983), 23.

Chapter 3: Caleb: Sustaining a Resilient Faith

1   Vance Havner, <u>By the Way: Meditation of a Christian Pilgrim</u> (Coppell, TX: Solid Christian Books, 2015), 14.
2   Tom Carter, comp. <u>Spurgeon at His Best,</u>(Grand Rapids: Baker Book House, 1988), 73.
3   I John 5:4 (ESV).

Chapter 4: Elijah: Overcoming the Urge to Quit

1 F. Deaville Walker, <u>William Carey: Missionary Pioneer, Statesman,</u> (Chicago: Moody Press, 1925), 42.
2 Galatians 6:9 (ESV).
3 John R. W. Stott, <u>The Gospel and the End of Time</u> (Dawners Grove, IL: InterVarsity Press, 1991), 42.

Chapter 5: Mary: Moving Beyond Impossible

1 Ken Gire "meditation" in Calvin Miller, ed. <u>The Book of Jesus</u>, (New York: Simon and Schuster, 1996), 166.
2 Lk 1:34, 37 (ESV).
3 Brant Pitre, <u>Jesus and the Jewish Roots of Mary</u>, (New York: Image/ Crown Publishing 2018), 97.

Chapter 6: John the Baptist: Staying the Course of Truth

1 Blaise Pascal, <u>Pensees</u> Sect. XIV Appendix: Political Fragments, # 864. This is a Scholar Select reprint of Pascal's 17th-century publication. It is now part of the Public Domain.
2 I Cor. 15:55 (NASB)
3 William Shakespeare's "Measure for Measure" ed. Stephen Orgel and A. R. Braunmuller, <u>The Complete Pelican Shakespeare</u> (New York: The Penguin Group, 2002), Act 1, Scene 4, line 80.

Chapter 7. Peter: Prevailing Against Shame

1 Curt Thompson, <u>The Soul of Shame, Retelling the Stories We Believe About Ourselves</u>, Downers Grove, IL: InterVarsity Press, 2015, p. 142.
2 Romans 8:1. (NASB)
3 Adam Hamilton, Simon Peter: <u>Flawed but Faithful Disciple</u>, (Nashville: Abingdon Press, 2018), 105.

Chapter 8: Paul: Combating the Sin of Racism

1   Benjamin Watson, <u>Under Our Skin: Getting Real about Race</u>, (Wheaton, IL: Tyndale House Publishing, 2015), 188.
2   I John 2:11 (ESV).
3   Tony Evans, <u>Oneness Embraced</u> (Chicago: Moody Press, 2011), 310.

END NOTES

Introduction: Holy Grit: The Will to Persevere

1   A. W. Tozer, The Divine Conquest (Wheaton I1: Tyndale Publishing Living Books edition, 1995) preface XV.
2   See Angela Duckworth, Grit: The Power of Passion and Perseverance, (New York: Scribner, 2016).
3   See Jon M. Jachimowicz, Andreas Wihler, Erica R. Bailey, and Adam D. Galinsky, "Why Grit Requires Perseverance and Passion to Positively Predict Performance" Proceedings of the National Academy of Sciences of the United States of America, October 2, 2018.
4   Duckworth, Grit, 275.
5   Jerry Bridges, The Pursuit of Holiness (Colorado Springs: NavPress, 2006), 10-11.
6   John Piper, A Godward Life (Sisters, Oregon: Multnomah Publishers, 1997), 39.
7   Sam Wellman, C.S. Lewis: Creator of Narnia, (Uhrichsville, Ohio: Barbour Publishing, 1979), 92.

Chapter 1: Abraham: Enduring a Severe Wait

1   Christopher Muther, "Instant Gratification is making us Perpetually Impatient," Boston Globe, Feb. 2, 2016, http://www.bostonglobe.com/lifestyle/2013/02/01/the-growing-culture-impatience (accessed Jan. 27, 2022).
2   Hebrews 11:8. (NASB)
3   Dean Register, "Points to Ponder," Reader's Digest, January 1987, 179.

4 "Management Consulting in the US," <u>IBIS World</u> July 30, 2022. (accessed Sept. 14, 2022).

5 Oscar Wilde, <u>A Woman of No Importance. </u>(London: Haymarket Theater, 1893), act 3.

6 Genesis 16.12. (NASB)

7 Genesis 17:18. (CSB)

8 Terry L. Brensinger, "nasah".נסה <u>New International Dictionary of Old Testament Theology and Exegesis</u>, ed. Willem A. VanGemeren vol. 3 (Grand Rapids: Zondervan Publishing House, 1997) by Terry L. Brensinger, pp. 111-113.

9 W. Garden Blaikie, <u>The Personal Life of David Livingstone</u>, (Westwood, NJ: Barbour and Company, 1986), 471.

10 Genesis 22:2. (ESV)

11 Victor P. Hamilton, <u>Genesis 18-50</u>, <u>The New International Commentary on the Old Testament</u> (Grand Rapids: Eerdmans Publishing, 1995), 101.

12 Paul Copan, <u>Is God a Moral Monster: Making Sense of the Old Testament God</u> (Grand Rapids: Baker Books, 2011), 48.

13 I Chron. 21:24 and 2 Chron 3:1. (ESV)

14 Heb. 11:19.(NASB)

15 C. S. Lewis, <u>The Screwtape Letters</u> (New York: Macmillan Publishing Inc., 1961), p. 47

16 Genesis 22:8, 12. (CSB)

17 John 1:29. (ESV)

18 Gen. 22:18. (ESV)

19 James 2:23. (ESV)

Chapter 2: Joseph: Finding a Way to Forgive

1 Jessica LeMasurier, "Sin to sell papal domain to porn" <u>CNN International.com</u> April 20, 2005, (accessed Oct 1, 2021).

2 Dianne Cole, *"The Healing Power of Forgiveness"* <u>Wall Street Journal</u>, March 20, 2106 (accessed Nov 1, 2021).

3 Isaiah 53:5. (ESV)

4 This is a lyric line from William Cowper's hymn <u>God Moves in a Mysterious Way.</u>

5 Gen. 37:4. (ESV)

6   A. H. Konkel שָׁנָא "sane" New International Dictionary of Old Testament Theology of Exegesis ed. Willem A. Van Gemeren, vol. 3 (Grand Rapids: Eerdmans 1997), 1256-1260.

7   Roland C. Warren, Bad Dads of the Bible (Grand Rapids: Zondervan, 2013), 63.

8   Alexander C. Jensen, Shawn D. Whitman, Karen L. Fingerman and Kira S. Birditt, "Life Still Isn't Fair: Parental Differential Treatment of Young Adult Siblings" Journal of Marriage and Family, 14 March 2013, Vo. 75 Issue 2 pp. 438-452.

9   Gen 37:18-24. (ESV)

10 Gen. 37:25 (ESV)

11 Richard E. Averboeck, טַבָּח "tabbach" in New International Dictionary of Old Testament Theololgy and Exegesis ed. Willem A. VanGemeren, vol 2 (Grand Rapids, Eerdmans 1997), 334-336.

12 Genesis 39:21. (ESV)

13 Mark Buchanan, Your God is Too Safe (Colorado Springs: Multnomah Books, 2001), 159.

14 Kenneth A. Matthews, The New American Commentary: An Exegetical and Theological Exposition of Holy Scripture vol. 1B "Genesis 11:27-50:26 (Nashville: Broadman and Holman, 2005), 761.

15 Gen. 42:9, 12,14,16. (ESV)

16 Henry Morris, The Genesis Record: A Scientific and Devotional Commentary of the Book of Beginning (Grand Rapids: Baker Books, 1990), 610.

17 I John 1:9. (NKJV)

18 John R. W. Stott, The Cross of Christ (Downers Grove: Intervarsity Press, 1986), 296.

19 See Byron Hollinshead, ed. I Wish I'd Been There (New York: Doubleday, 2006).

20 Gen 45:5; Gen. 45:7; Gen. 45:8; Gen 45:9. (ESV)

21 Gen. 50:20. (ESV)

22 Arnold A. Dallimore, A Heart Set Feee: The Life of Charles Wesley (Westchester, IL: Crossway Books, 1988), 175-82.

23 Ibid, 180.

24 See Calvin Miller, Life is Mostly Edges, A Memoir (Nashville: Thomas Nelson, 2008), p. 353-354. In our conversation, Calvin reaffirmed that he wanted me to preach his funeral service which he noted in his memoir. I fulfilled that bittersweet vow on August 22, 2012.

25 Charles Haddon Spurgeon, "David Encouraging Himself in God," June 26, 1881. The Metropolitan Tabernacle Pulpit, vol 27 (London: Alabaster, Pasmore and Sons, 1882), 373.

Chapter 3: Caleb: Sustaining a Resilient Faith

1 "Pilot Sucked Out of Plane, Hangs Tight til Landing," Los Angeles Times www.latimes.com Sept. 3, 1987. (accessed May 8, 2022).

2 Ephesians 3:20. (ESV)

3 Duane A. Garrett, A Commentary of Exodus (Grand Rapids: Kregel Publications, 2014), 203.

4 Philip J. Budd, Numbers Word Biblical Commentary (Waco, TX: Word Books Publisher, 1984), 145.

5 James S. Stewart, A Faith to Proclaim (New York: Scribner's Sons, 1953), 65-66. Stewart's anecdote is an embellished variation of the documented original found in the Columbia Chess Chronicle "Anecdote of Morphy" Aug 18, 1888 Vol. 3, p. 60 Paul Morphy was the chess master who solved the checkmate enigma.

6 Numbers 14:24; 32:11; Deut. 1:36; Josh. 143:8,9,14. (ESV)

7 Numbers 14:24. (NASB)

8 R.Dennis Cole, Numbers The New American Commentary (Nashville: Broadman and Holman, 2000), 233. Although Cole cited the "my servant' epithet God assigned to Moses and Caleb, I am confident that he knows it was also attributed to Abraham in Gen. 26:24.

9 Robert L. Hubbard, Jr. Joshua The NIV Application Commentary (Grand Rapids: Zondervan), 405.

10 Elisabeth Elliot, Shadow of the Almighty: The Life and Testament of Jim Elliot (New York: Harper One, 1979), 108.

11 Mary Ann Norbom and Jane Briggs – Bunting, "A Flight Plan to Glory Ends Tragically for Bomber, the Official Bald Eagle of the 1984 Olympics" Aug 13, 1984 People. com>archive. (accessed: June 16, 2022).

12 I borrowed this phrase from Jeff Manion's insightful book, The Land Between: Finding God in Difficult Transitions (Grand Rapids: Zondervan, 2010), 13-21.

13 Gene Smith, Lee and Grant:A Dual Biography: (New York: Meridian Books, 1984), 199-200.

14 George Smith, The Life of William Carey: Shoemaker and Missionary (London: John Murray, 1887), 35.

15   Timothy George, Faithful Witness: The Life and Mission of William Carey (Birmingham, AL: New Hope, 1991), 173.

16   F. Deaville Walker, William Carey: Missionary Pioneer and Statesman (Chicago: Moody Press, 1925), 42.

17   John C. Maxwell, The 21 Irrefutable Laws of Leadership (Nashville: Thomas Nelson Publishers, 1998), 133-134.

18   Joshua 14:6-14. (ESV)

19   John Steinbeck, Travels with Charley in Search of America (New York: Penguin Books, 2017), 19-20.

20   Joshua 14:10-11. (ESV)

Chapter 4: Elijah: Overcoming the Urge to Quit

1   Cal Ripken, Jr. and James Dale, Just Show Up: And Other Enduring Values from Baseball's Iron Man, (New York: Harper Publishers, 2019), 82.

2   I Kings 16:31. (ESV)

3   I Kings 17:1. (ESV).

4   Robin Wakely, צרף Zareph" in New International Dictionary of Old Testament Theology and Exegesis, ed. Willem A. VanGemeren, vol 3 Grand Rapids: Eerdmans 1997), 847-853.

5   I Kings 17:20-21. (NASB)

6   I Jn.5:14. (NKJV)

7   Mary Beth Chapman and Ellen Vaughn, Choosing to See: A Journey of Struggle and Hope (Grand Rapids: Revell Publishing, 2010), 145.

8   C.S. Lewis, Christian Reflections (Grand Rapids: Eerdmans Publishing, 1968), 33.

9   I Kings 18:21 (ESV)

10   I Kings 18:37-38 (ESV)

11   I Kings 18:43 (ESV)

12   Lyle Dorsett, A Passion for God: The Spiritual Journey of A. W. Tozer, (Chicago: Moody Publishers, 2008, 123, 143-144, 159-160.

13   Rudolph W. Heizne, Reform and Conflict: The Baker History of the Church, vol. 4 (Grand Rapids: Baker Books, 2005), 188-190. See also Philip Schaff, History of the Christian Church, vol. 7 (Grand Rapids: Eerdmans Publishing, 1910) 68-70.

14   Norman P. Grubb, C.T. Studd: Cricketer and Pioneer, (London: Lutterworth Press, 1933), 166.

15 Ibid, 231-233.

16 James 5:17.(NASB)

17 I Jn. 4:18. (CSB)

18 George S. Patton, Jr. War As I Knew It, ed. Beatrice Ayer Patton (New York: Houghton Mifflin Company, 1947), 402.

19 Calvin Miller, Into the Depths of God (Minneapolis: Bethany House, 2000) 210.

20 I Kings 19:4. (NKJV)

21 I Kings 19:10. (ESV)

22 Theodore Roosevelt, "Citizenship in a Republic" in Theodore Roosevelt: Letters and Speeches (New York: Penguin Putnam Inc., 2004) 781-892.

23 Matt. 11:28-29. (ESV)

24 I Kings 19:9 (The Hebrew text consists of 5 words: "What to you here, Elijah").

25 Philip Graham Ryken, I Kings, Reformed Expository Commentary Series (Phillipsburg, NJ: P&R Publishing 2011), 530.

26 I Kings 19:12. (Notice the variations among the translations: ESV, NASB, NKJV, CSB).

27 Donald J. Wiseman, I and 2 Kings, The Tyndale Old Testament Commentaries (Downers Grove: Inter-Varsity Press, 1993), 173.

28 I Kings 19:15-17. (ESV)

29 I Corinthians 15:58. (NASB)

Chapter 5: Mary: Moving Beyond Impossible

1 David Lyle Jeffrey, "Hail Mary", Christian History issue 103, 2012:11.

2 Scot McKnight, The Real Mary: Why Evangelical Christians Can Embrace the Mother of Jesus (Brewster, MA; Paraclete Press, 2007), 19.

3 The New York Times, October 9, 1903, p. 6.

4 David McCullough, The Wright Brothers (New York: Simon and Schuster, 2015), 107.

5 Luke 1:46. (CSB)

6 James R. Edwards, The Gospel According to Luke, Pillar New Testament Commentary, (Grand Rapids: Wm. B. Eerdmans Publishing 2015), 56.

7 Matthew 1:19. (CSB)

8 Frederick Dale Bruner, Matthew: A Commentary, vol. 1 Matthew 1-12 rev. ed. (Grand Rapids: Wm. BG. Eerdmans Publishing, 2004), 48.

9 Luke 1:38. (ESV)

10 Fleming Rutledge, <u>Advent: The Once and Future Coming of Jesus Christ</u>, (Grand Rapids: Wm. B. Eerdmans Publishing Co., 2018), 388.

11 James Dobson, <u>Parenting Isn't for Cowards</u> (Waco: Word Books, 1987).

12 Luke 2:41-51. (ESV)

13 Cleon L. Rogers Jr. and Cleon L. Rogers III, <u>The New Linguistic and Exegetical Key to the Greek New Testament</u> (Grand Rapids: Zondervan Publishing House, 1998), 114.

14 John 2:1-11. (ESV)

15 D. A. Carson, <u>The Gospel According to John</u> The Pillar New Testament Commentary (Grand Rapids: Wm. B. Eerdmans Publishing, 1991), 168.

16 Luke 3:23. (ESV)

17 Leon Morris, <u>The Gospel According to John</u>, The New International Commentary on the New Testament rev. ed. (Grand Rapids: Wm. B. Eerdmans Publishing, 1995), 158.

18 John 2:5. (ESV)

19 Mark 3:20-21. (ESV)

20 Mark 3:33-35. (ESV)

21 John 7:5. (ESV)

22 Luke 2:35. (ESV

23 John 8:32. (ESV)

24 John Piper, <u>Seeing and Savoring Jesus Christ</u>, (Wheaton: Crossway Books, 2004), 60.

25 Religious leaders included elders, pharisees, scribes and the high priest. See Matthew 26:3-4, 14-16 Luke 22:2-5 and John 11:45-57.

26 Michard Card, "Why" in <u>Known by the Scars</u> track #6, Sparrow Records, 1985.

27 John 19:5. (ESV)

28 John 19:6. (ESV)

29 2 Cor 5:21. (ESV)

30 John 19:39. (The NASB says one hundred pounds, but the ESV says seventy-five pounds).

31 Luke 23:55. (CSB)

32 Acts 1:14 (The last mention of Mary in the New Testament is Acts 1:14).

33 Luke 1:47. (ESV)

34 Tim Perry, <u>Mary For Evangelicals: Toward an Understanding of the Mother of Our Lord</u> (Downers Grove, IL: InterVarsity Press, 2006), 293.

Chapter 6: John the Baptist: Staying the Course of Truth

1   Jeff Wilser, "10 Genius Acts of Awesomeness" <u>Mental Floss</u> July/ August 2015, 44. (A Short Movie titled "Manjhi the Mountain Man" was released in 2015).

2   Luke 1:80. (ESV)

3   Luke 1:5. (ESV)

4   Nicholas Carr, "How Smartphones Hijack Our Minds" <u>Wall Street Journal</u>, October 6, 2017. (accessed Aug. 14, 2022).

5   Wordsworth, William, "The World Is Too Much With Us" Poetry Foundation, https// www.PoetryFoundation.org (accessed Aug. 10, 2022).

6   Henry David Thoreau. <u>Walden: Or Life in the Woods</u> (Floyd, Va: Sublime Books, 2015), 67.

7   A.W. Tozer, <u>The Pursuit of God</u> (Camp Hill, PA: Christian Publications, Inc. 1982), 23.

8   Matthew 3:4 and Mark 1:6. (ESV)

9   Leviticus 11:22. (ESV)

10   Craig S. Keener, <u>A Commentary on the Gospel of Matthew</u> (Grand Rapids: Wm. B. Eerdmans Publishing, 1999), 116.

11   Calvin Miller, <u>The Table of Inwardness</u> (Downers Grove, IL: InterVarsity Press, 1984), 17.

12   C.S. Lewis, <u>The Voyage of the Dawn Treader</u> (New York: Harper Collins Publishers, 1952), 108-110.

13   Alexander Whyte, <u>Bible Characters</u>, rep. ed. (Grand Rapids: Zondervan Publishing, 1973), 27 in N.T. section.

14   Deuteronomy 16:16 states that all males were obligated to attend three feasts: the Feast of Unleavened Bread, the Feast of Weeks, and the Feast of Booths.

15   Jn. 1:6. (ESV)

16   Jn. 1:23 and Isa. 40:3. (ESV)

17   Mt. 11:9. (NASB)

18   Jn. 3:11. (ESV)

19   Mt. 11:11. (ESV)

20   Marcus L. Loane, <u>John the Baptist as Witness and Martyr</u> (Grand Rapids: Zondervan Publishing, 1968) 105.

21   John Nolland, <u>The Gospel of Matthew: A Commentary on the Greek Text</u> (Grand Rapids: William B. Eerdmans, 2005), 457.

22   Martin Brecht, <u>Martin Luther: His Road to Reformation</u> trans. James L. Schaff (Philadelphia: Fortress Press, 1985), 460.

23 Phillips Brooks, <u>Lectures on Preaching</u> (New York: E. P. Dutton and Company, 1898), 59.

24 Billy Graham, <u>Just As I Am: An Autobiography</u> (San Francisco: Harper Collins Publishers, Inc. 1997), 257.

25 Ibid, 259.

26 William Whiston, trans. <u>The Works of Josephus.</u>, (Peabody, MA: Hendrickson Publishers, 1987), 484.

27 Jn. 1:29. (ESV)

28 Ibid.

29 29 Jn. 1:34. (ESV)

30 Robert H. Mounce, <u>The Essential Nature of New Testament Preaching</u> (Grand Rapids: Wm. B, Eerdmans Publishing, 1960), 21.

31 Grant R. Osborne, <u>Matthew</u>, Zondervan Exegetical Commentary of the New Testament, ed. Clinton E. Arnold (Grand Rapids: Zondervan, 2010), 113.

32 Lk 3:8. (ESV)

33 Lk 3:11-14. (ESV)

34 Deitrich Bonhoeffer, <u>Life Together</u>, (San Francisco: Harper Collins, 1954), 126.

35 Matt. 3:15. (ESV)

36 Jn. 3:27. (ESV)

37 Jn. 3:29. (ESV)

38 Jn. 3:30. (ESV)

39 J. T. Keith, "Remembering Walter 'Sweetness' Peyton, 23 years after his death" <u>Mississippi Clarion Ledger</u> Nov. 2, 2022, (accessed Nov. 20, 2022)

40 Herbert Lockyer, <u>Last Words of Saints and Sinners</u>, (Grand Rapids: Kregel Publications, 1983), 81.

41 Mark 6:19. (ESV)

42 Flavius Josephus, The Works of Josephus: trans. William Whiston (Peabody MA: Hendrickson Publishers, 1987, 484.

43 Matt. 11:3. (ESV)

44 Alister McGrath, <u>Doubting: Growing Through the Uncertainties of Faith</u> (Downers Grove, IL: InterVarsity Press, 2006), 145.

45 Isaiah 26:19; 29:18; 35:5-6; 61:1-2 (ESV)

Chapter 7. Peter: Prevailing Against Shame

1   Stephen Orgel and A. R. Braunmuller, eds. "The Tragedy of Julius Caesar," act 3, scene 2 in <u>William Shakespeare: The Complete Works</u> (New York: Penguin Putnjam Inc., 2002), 1321.

2   Lee Jerry Tarde "Roberto DeVicenzo and 1968 Masters: "When The Game Held Its Head in Its Hands" <u>Golf Digest.com</u> Retrieved July 30, 2021. See John Moriello, "Masters Disasters: Roberto DeVicezo's Scorecard Gaffe Will Always be Augusta's Worst Mistake" <u>Sportscasting. com</u> April 11, 2022.

3   Brene' Brown, <u>The Gifts of Imperfection</u> 10th Anniv. ed. (New York: Random House, 2020), 54.

4   Sandra D. Wilson, <u>Released from Shame</u> rev. ed. (Downers Grove, IL: InterVarsity Press, 2002), 23.

5   Matt. 4:19 and John 21:22. (ESV)

6   Matt. 26:33,35. (ESV)

7   Matt. 26:58. (ESV)

8   Frederick Williams Danker, ed <u>A Greek-English Lexicon of the New Testament and other Early Christian Literature rev.</u> 3rd ed. (Chicago: The University of Chicago Press, 2000), "ἐμβλέπω," 321.

9   Michael Card, <u>A Fragile Stone: The Emotional Life of Simon Peter</u>, (Downers Grove, IL: InterVarsity Press, 2003), 111.

10 Luke 22:31 (ESV)

11 Respectively in order: Mt. 13:38-39; Jn 12:31; Jn 8:44 (ESV)

12 I Peter 5:8-9. (ESV)

13 Luke 22:32 (ESV)

14 John 21:7. (ESV)

15 David W. Gill, <u>Peter the Rock: Extraordinary Insights from an Ordinary Man</u> (Downers Grove, Il: InterVarsity Press, 1986)126.

16 John 21:15. (ESV)

17 A.T. Robertson, <u>Epochs in the Life of Simon Peter</u> (New York: Charles Scribner's Sons, 1943), 168.

18 Edward W. Klink III, <u>John</u>, Zondervan Exegetical Commentary on the New Testament, ed. Clinton E. Arnold (Grand Rapids: Zondervan, 2016), 914.

19 Leon Morris, <u>Testaments of Love: A Study of Love in the Bible</u> (Grand Rapids: William B. Eerdmans Publishing, 1981), 181.

20 I Corinthians 13:13 and Matthew 22:37-38.

21 John 21:18. (ESV)

22 Andreas J. Kostenberger, <u>John</u>, Baker Exegetical Commentary on the New Testament (Grand Rapids: Baker Academic, 2004), 598.

23 I Peter 2:21. (ESV)

24 2 Peter 3:18. (ESV)

Chapter 8: Paul: Combating the Sin of Racism

1 The wickedness of slavery is well documented in many sources. I am indebted to James L. Gorman, Jeff W. Childers, and Mark Hamilton, eds., <u>Slavery's Long Shadow: Race & Reconciliation in American Christianity</u> (Grand Rapids: Eerdmans, 2019) and Robert William Fogel, <u>Without Consent or Contract: The Rise and Fall of American Slavery</u> (New York: W.W. Norton and Company, 1989) for their exemplary resources.

2 Cornelius Plantinga, Jr., <u>Not the Way It's Supposed to Be: A Breviary of Sin</u> (Grand Rapids: Eerdmans, 1995), 62.

3 2 Corinthians 5:18-19 (ESV)

4 Ivor J. Davidson, <u>The Birth of the Church</u>, The Baker History of the Church, vol. 1, ed Tim Dowley (Grand Rapids: Baker Books), 19.

5 Brian Rapske, <u>Paul in Roman Custody</u>, The Book of Acts in Its First Century Setting, vol. 3, ed. Bruce W. Winter (Grand Rapids: Wm. B. Eerdmans, 1994), 73-74.

6 F.F. Bruce, <u>Paul: Apostle of the Heart Set Free, (Grand Rapids: Wm. B. Eerdmans,</u> 1977), 35.

7 Paul L. Maier, <u>In The Fullness of Time</u> (Grand Rapids: Kregel Publications, 1997), 246

8 Acts 22:3,28 and Phil. 3:5 (ESV)

9 Acts 7:58 and Acts 22:20 (ESV)

10 Eckhard, J. Schnabel, <u>Paul and the Early Church</u>, Early Christian Mission vol. 2 (Downers Grove: InterVarsity Press, 2004), 940.

11 Ronald F. Hock, <u>The Social Context of Paul's Ministry</u> (Philadelphia: Fortress Press, 1980), 27.

12 David W. J. Gill "Acts and the Urban Elites" in <u>Graeco-Roman Setting</u>, The Book of Acts in Its First Century Setting, vol. 2 eds. David W. J. Gill and Conrad Gempf (Grand Rapids: Wm. B. Eerdmans, 1994), 106.

13 Everett Ferguson, <u>Backgrounds of Early Christianity</u> 3rd ed. (Grand Rapids. Wm. B. Eerdmans, 2003), 58.

14 J. Albert Harrill "Paul and Slavery" in <u>Paul in the Greco-Roman World</u> ed. J. Paul Sampley (Harrisburg, PA: Trinity Press International, 2003), 579.

15 Arthur A. Rupprecht, "slave/slavery' in <u>Dictionary of Paul and His Letters</u> eds. G. F. Hawthorne, Ralph P. Martin and Daniel G. Reid (Downers Grove: InterVarsity Press, 1993), 881.

16 S. Scott Bartchy, "Slaves and Slavery in the Roman World" in <u>The World of the New Testament: Cultural, Social, and Historical Contexts</u> eds. Joel B. Green and Lee Martin McDonald (Grand Rapids: Baker Publishing, 2013), 172.

17 J. Albert Harrill, "Paul and Slavery" in <u>Paul in the Greco-Roman World</u>, 579.

18 Kenneth Scott Latourette, <u>A History of Christianity</u> (New York: Harper and Row, 1953), 71.

19 Galatians 2:11-16. (CSB)

20 Timothy George, <u>Galatians</u>, The New American Commentary: An Exegetical and Theological Exposition of Holy Scripture, vol. 30. (Nashville: Broadman and Holman, 1994), 182.

21 Galatians 3:28. (ESV)

22 I understand the nuanced differences in Pauline Chronology, but I am using the chronology presented in Andreas J. Kostenberger, L. Scott Kellum, and Charles L. Quarles, <u>The Cradle, The Cross, and The Crown: An Introduction to the New Testament</u> (Nashville: B & H Publishing, 2009).

23 Frederick Douglass, <u>Narrative of the Life of Frederick Douglass, an American Slave</u>, ed. Ira Dworkin (New York: Penguin Books, 1982), 110. Originally published by the Anti-Slavery Office in 1845.

24 Acts 17:6. (ESV)

25 I Cor 8:10-12; 10:19:21; 2 Cor 6:15-7:1. (ESV)

26 I Cor. 7:21 a. (ESV)

27 I Cor 7:21 b. (ESV)

28 <u>Bartchy</u> "Slaves and Slavery in the Roman World," 174.

29 Roy E. Ciampa and Brian S. Rosner, <u>The First Letter to the Corinthians</u>, The Pillar New Testament Commentary (Grand Rapids: Wm. B. Eerdmans, 2010), 322.

30 Lisa M. Bowens, <u>African American Readings of Paul: Reception, Resistance, and Transformation</u> (Grand Rapids: Wm. B. Eerdmans), 49-58.

31 Richard E. Oster, Jr. "Ephesus" <u>The Anchor Bible Dictionary</u> vol 2, ed David Noel Freedman (New York: Doubleday, 1992), 545.

32 Harold W. Hoehner, <u>Ephesians: An Exegetical Commentary</u> (Grand Rapids: Baker Academic, 2002), 379.

33 A lengthy defense of Onesimus being sent by Philemon can be found in David W. Pao. Colossians and Philemon Zondervan Exegetical Commentary on the New Testament ed. Clinton E. Arnold (Grand Rapids: Zondervan Publishing 2012), 345-346.

34 Philippians 4:22 (NASB)

35 Miroslav Volf, Exclusion and Embrace: A Theological Exploration of Identity, Otherness, and Reconciliation, rev. ed. (Nashville: Abingdon Press, 2019), 203.

36 John M. Perkins, One Blood: Parting Words to the Church on Race and Love (Chicago: Moody Publishers, 2018), 52.

37 Wayne Grudem, Christian Ethics: An Introduction to Biblical Moral Reasoning (Wheaton, IL: Crossway 2018), 642.

38 John Stonestreet & Brett Kunkle, A Practical Guide to Culture (Colorado Springs: David C. Cook, 2017), 280-283.

39 Thaddeus J. Williams, Confronting Injustice Without Compromising the Truth (Grand Rapids: Zondervan Academic, 2020), 117-118.

40 Scott David Allen, Why Social Justice is Not Biblical Justice (Grand Rapids: Creds House Publishers, 2020), 105.

41 Martin Luther King, Jr., Strength To Love (Boston: Beacon Press, 1963), 47.

42 I Corinthians 13:13. (ESV)

Postscript

1   The Two Towers, directed by Peter Jackson, 2002. Scene "The Tales that Really Mattered." Adapted and embellished from J.R.R. Tolkien, Lord of the Rings: The Two Towers (New York: Houghton Mifflin Company, 1954, renewed 1994), 320-321.

Made in the USA
Columbia, SC
24 July 2023

20799083R00136